> **"Hope is the thing with feathers that perches in the soul and sings the tune without the words and never stops at all."**
>
> Emily Dickinson[1]

Copyright

ISBN   978-1-952359-37-8   (paperback)
ISBN   978-1-952359-38-5   (ebook)

For More Information
About the Life Planning Series:

www.lifeplanningtools.com

Life Planning Series
by J. S. Wellman

Choose The Right Words

Filter your speech for effective personal growth.

LIFE PLANNING SERIES
J.S. WELLMAN

Extra-mile Publishing

Free PDF

Wise Decision-Making

[Get the ebook version for 99 cents]

We want to give you a <u>free</u> copy of:

Wise Decision-Making:
You can make good choices.

This book will help you make good decisions in your life, career, family . . .

Free PDF:
www.lifeplanningtools.link/howtodecide

eBook for 99 cents:
https://www.amazon.com/dp/B09SYGWRVL/

Ebook

Free PDF

Improve your life!

Life Planning Handbook

Obtain a copy of the Handbook if you want to be guided in developing your own personal Life Plan.

Purpose of a Life Plan

- To help you develop direction in your life.
- To encourage you to make good decisions.
- To help build your life on proven life principles.
- To help you establish goals for your life.
- To identify what you hope to accomplish in life.
- To help you make the most of every opportunity.

Life Planning Series

Life Planning Handbook

Go to www.amazon.com/dp/1952359325
to get your copy now.

Don't wait to have a better life!

Table of Contents

Message From Author

The general purpose of this book and the Life Planning Series is to encourage you to pursue actions and character traits that will produce your best life. The book series will address 15 to 25 significant activities or traits that help people improve their lives and live a better life.

First, understand that you can improve or acquire high personal character and outstanding habits, no matter how good or bad your life may be at this moment. Good personal character and good life habits can be achieved. They will allow you to live a better life.

Second, know that you don't have to read all the books in this series to make a significant change or improvement in your life. Find the books that focus on the areas of your life that you want to improve.

Third, know that this is a progressive journey. You don't need to climb the highest mountain immediately. You may just want to learn more about the basic principles of good character. This series will provide you with a foundation for decisions relative to your lifestyle, goals, priorities, and commitments.

Fourth, know that the key to developing high character and making good decisions in your life is *intentionality*. The Life Planning Series will help you identify the path you want to travel, but you will need to be intentional about walking that path if you want to make progress toward the goal of living a better life.

Fifth, know that change will require making good decisions, establishing important core values in your life, setting priorities, and making commitments. This book will help you identify the values in life that will produce high personal character and good habits.

Sixth, know that this series, and the entire Life Planning product line, are designed to help you smooth out the path for your life journey. We will provide the tools you need to make the best choices and decisions for traveling your life path.

Seventh, remember that all actions (both words and deeds) have consequences. These consequences will impact you and all those around you. Read carefully Chapter 2 on "Consequences," which is particularly important for your understanding when making decisions.

Lastly, the very simple formula for success is: "*Decide you want to do it and work at it regularly*."

This book will give you guidance and we will even provide coaching if you want it. If you want to improve your life, just commit and carry through. We are here to help!

Decide to be the very best you can be!

Life Planning Series

Before you read this book it will be useful if you have an understanding of the purpose and focus of the entire Life Planning Series. The series will examine major personal characteristics, traits, and habits that are fundamental influencers in life. Each book will include a Life Analysis focused on the subject of the book and then help you develop a plan to improve _that particular area_ in your life. In addition, we can provide coaching assistance for those who want hands-on help.

Those who want to develop a _total life plan_ can do that by acquiring our _Life Planning Handbook_. For details, see the "Next Steps" section at the end of this book and the Ad Page describing the Hand book following that section.

LIFE PLANNING SERIES

It is our objective in these books to help you choose the best path and give you tools to make good decisions in your life journey. The series is divided into five different categories to help organize the books and make it easy for you to find related subjects.

All the books will be meaningful to a general reading audience, but because the Christian viewpoint brings a different approach to many of these subjects and concepts, that perspective will be addressed in a separate Christian Wisdom Series. That series is intended for

Christians but others may find the first book in that series particularly interesting because it is focused on the proverbs of the Bible. The Christian Wisdom Series will be published after the Life Planning Series is complete.

The initial plan is to publish books on the following topics:

Subjects		Life Principle
Personal Character:		
Integrity*	honesty, truth, compromise/standing firm, justice, fairness	Be honest, live with integrity, and base Life on truth.
Reputation	respect, responsibility, sincerity	Earn the respect of others.
Leadership	power, decisiveness, courage, influence, loyalty	Lead well and be a loyal follower.
Identity/Self-Image	humor, being genuine, authenticity, confidence	Be confident in who you are.
Wisdom	discernment, correction, folly, foolishness	Seek knowledge, understanding, and wisdom.
Personal Relationships:		
Friends*	Friends, associates, acquaintances	Choose your friends wisely.
Family	Honor, parenting, discipline	Honor your family.
Love	Love is . . .	Love one another.
Compassion	humility, mercy, goodness, kindness	Treat others as you would want to be treated.
Forgiveness	reject grudges and revenge	Forgive others; do not hold grudges or take revenge.

Self-Control:

Speech*		Guard your speech.
Anger	self-control, self-discipline, patience	Always under control.
Addiction	moderation, life balance	Live a life of balance and moderation, not excess.
Immorality	temptation	Set high moral standards.

Work Ethic:

Diligence*	apathy, laziness, perseverance, resilience, energy	Be diligent and a hard worker.
Trustworthiness	dependability, reliability, responsibility	Be trustworthy, dependable, and reliable.
Skills	curiosity, knowledge, education, abilities	Seek excellence; strive to do everything well.

Wealth:

Money*	wealth, poverty	Make sound financial choices.
Gratitude	generosity, thankfulness, gratefulness	Be thankful, grateful, and generous.

*The first subject listed under each of the categories above make up the Primary Life Principles.

After the initial launch of the first five books in the series, the books will be published in 4 to 8 week intervals.

LIFE PLANNING HANDBOOK

The purpose of this book is to produce a total and complete Life Plan for all the major activities in your life:

1. Life Principles and Character Attributes
2. Habits

3. Friends and Family Relationships
4. Work and Work Ethic
5. Education
6. Community Service
7. Money and Wealth
8. Health
9. Spiritual

The planning process in this book will examine your skills and abilities, your personal life values, core values, priorities, and commitments. The book will help you identify your life goals and create action steps to achieve those goals. It also includes additional help and tools in the Appendix. Coaching assistance is available for those who want additional help.

These products and services will generate purpose, direction, and growth in your life.

Choose the subjects and products that work for you and your needs.

PRELUDE

Character is like a tree and reputation like its shadow.
The shadow is what we think of it;
the tree is the real thing.
Abraham Lincoln[2]

The primary purpose of this book is to inform, encourage, and inspire readers to guard their speech or be careful of their words. We can learn a wealth of practical wisdom for daily living from common sense, wise sayings, logical thinking, and quotes from wise people.

The second and equally important purpose is to help you develop a plan that will assist you in implementing change in your life. The latter portion of this book is an easy-to-follow planning process for implementing that change.

The third purpose is our hope that you will pass it on. It is our desire that you will not only obtain this knowledge, but pass it on to others – particularly friends, children, grandchildren, or students.

An African proverb says, *"Don't spend all day rejoicing on your bench. When you pray, move your feet!"* The message of this proverb Is that if you want to accomplish something, nothing will happen if you're sitting on your bench all day. Growth and improvement, including living a better life, require action and intentionality. The good news is that you can use the information in this book and in the Life Planning Series to acquire knowledge that will help you follow a path to a better life.

Intentionality with a plan is the foundation for making progress!

Chapter 1

INTRODUCTION

Know your core values,
because they will drive your life.

CORE VALUES OF THE LIFE PLANNING SERIES

The Life Planning tools are developed around the following ten core values and principles:

1. Wise sayings, parables, proverbs, common sense, and street smarts provide an underlying foundation for gaining knowledge, understanding, and wisdom.

2. Honesty, integrity, and living a life based on truth are the foundational character traits for achieving a life of hope and contentment. They are the cornerstones to living a better life.

3. There are five <u>Primary</u> Life Principles:

- be honest, live with integrity, and base your life on truth,
- choose your friends wisely,
- choose your words carefully,
- be a diligent and hard worker, and
- do not love money or worship wealth.

4. Life change is possible. You can make positive changes and expect good results to follow. All choices have consequences.

5. It is not necessary to change a large number of character traits in order to achieve significant life improvement. Changing a few key areas can have a major impact on your quality of life.

6. The key to making any life change is *intentionality*.

7. Perfection is not possible, but if we aim for it, we can achieve significant results. Nothing will be attained if we do not try.

8. We will be open about the difficulties, barriers, and walls that one might experience in implementing life change. But barriers can be torn down.

9. The ultimate purpose in this series is to develop an effective plan for improving life circumstances. It is not our intent to provide lengthy textbooks on the particular subjects. Our presentation of the text material will be limited to what you need to know in order to develop an effective plan to improve your life.

10. Life is a progressive journey requiring good choices and a solid foundation for the future. Time is needed to implement change. Patience and perseverance will be necessary to achieve the desired results.

CUSTOMER CHARACTERISTICS

The ideal readers for our Life Planning products are people who:

- want to learn more about the subject of personal growth and self-improvement,

- want to live a good life, live at peace, be content, or have a successful life,
- want to dig more deeply into the meaning of living a good life,
- may be confused, have a history of bad choices, or are living in chaos,
- are feeling overwhelmed or discouraged,
- desire to change or improve their life, or
- want to learn how to make good or better decisions.

PERSONAL GROWTH

We will encourage you to make good choices and improve your life. This process is often referred to as personal growth. Some might call it self-help. However you think of it, our objective is to help you improve your life through the use of widely accepted life principles.

There are many good reasons for pursuing personal growth in life. We have already mentioned several in the preceding pages. Here are a few more:

- to find personal peace, meaning, and purpose;
- to gain more control over life circumstances;
- to be more effective in certain skills, abilities or decisions;
- to become more disciplined;
- to change an attitude or overcome a negative outlook;
- to expand potential horizons;
- to open new avenues of understanding; and
- to change certain outcomes in your life.

For the purpose of living your best life, you may only need help focusing on the right things. You may just need guidance in finding things you can tweak to make a few changes in your lifestyle. You may want a clearer vision of your goals. Or you may want to do some serious work on some particular aspect of your life. Our Life Planning products will help you achieve any of these desires.

BARRIERS TO PERSONAL GROWTH

Our commitment to the truth requires that we point out possible barriers that would keep you from achieving a better life. They can be overcome if you are intentional, but understand that you may encounter the following barriers:

- APATHY: You are not a self-starter and you tend to lack discipline. You are generally comfortable with your present life and find change frightening. Your commitment level is not high and change may seem to be too much work.

    Intentionality is the key to overcoming apathy. The starting point is desire. You must want to make something happen. The solution is to say "yes" to change and allow this book to guide your thoughts and actions toward living a better life.

- BUSY LIFE: You are too busy. You have no time. Your calendar is already too full.

    This reason comes up again and again as a serious deterrent to achieving any goal.

19

People are just extremely busy today. Life is too full. We are trying to find happiness and joy in doing things. We never stop to think, reflect, or meditate on life. Being too busy and the unwise use of our time are the biggest hurdles for completing any task. The solution is to change your priorities and your calendar.

- FEAR: You are afraid of taking risk, you fear embarrassment, or you are afraid you don't have the necessary skills to achieve any meaningful results. You are afraid it won't really work and you will have invested time that will be lost. You may be afraid to admit you need help!

    If you fear that it might not work we would encourage you to look at it in a more positive way. The solution is to think about what might be possible if you commit to this as passionately as you work at the other things you love.

- PEER PRESSURE: You might be considered a loser and be shunned by your group if they found out.

    It is true that peer pressure can be very hard to deal with. If you discover that your core values are in conflict with those of your friends and associates, you will ultimately face some difficult decisions. A better life will be lived when your core values match those of your close friends, particularly in the important areas of character, ethics, and moral standards. The solution is to choose your friends carefully.

Yes, there are barriers, but they can be overcome. The purpose of the Life Planning Series is to address important areas of life that are worthy of your time and effort. Again, there can be barriers, and you should be aware of them so you can determine how to overcome them.

Barriers can be overcome and torn down!

TIPS FOR OVERCOMING BARRIERS

Difficulties and barriers can be overcome if you want to find a solution. It's a lot easier to make changes in life if you are not doing it alone or if you are receiving guidance and help. In addition to our books and products we suggest finding someone to join you in your quest for a better life. If you cannot find someone to participate with you, find someone you can meet with weekly or periodically to discuss your progress, your difficulties, your needs, and most of all your successes.

Here are six effective ways to overcome barriers:

1. Recognize that many barriers are just excuses.
2. Recruit a support person (true friend) to hold you accountable (meet once a week).
3. Recruit others to do it with you. Push each other.

4. Do not expect change, improvement, or miracles overnight.
5. Recruit support and understanding from your family (spouse, children, or siblings).
6. If time is a hurdle – work it out. Adjust your priorities.

Alternatively, we will provide personal coaching for any parts of the plan. See Appendix C at the end of this book for information about our Coaching Assistance.

LUCK

Don't place any hope in luck. Generally luck has very little to do with favorable or unfavorable results. You can get lucky and win a card game or a lottery, but your abilities, skills, and strengths are not the result of luck. Yes, you can have God-given skills and abilities, but much of what you accomplish in life is the result of hard work and diligence, not luck.

Our lives will be the result of decisions we make and the consequences of those decisions. If you decide you want to be a plumber and you go to school and get the proper training and then intern with a licensed plumber, it is not luck that after ten years you have a successful plumbing business. The success was the result of planning, hard work, and dedication to a goal.

Thinking that one has to be lucky to achieve success is misguided.

TIPS YOU COULD USE

a. Underline, circle, or highlight the 1 to 3 tips above that you think could make the most impact if you implemented them in your life. You will revisit these choices at the end of the book in the Planning section.

b. There may be other things that you think would make a difference. Write them below:

_____

_____

_____

_____

In reality barriers are just excuses!

Chapter 2

CONSEQUENCES

Mess with the bull and one usually gets the horns.
Latin American saying[3]

GENERAL

Consequences are a vital concept in our understanding of making good choices and setting goals to have a successful life. Thus, this chapter on consequences will appear in each of the books in the Life Planning Series. You have complete freedom to choose what you want to do. But, you cannot choose the consequences. Thus, it is important to manage and control your actions because the result of poor choices could be a disaster.

You and I will bear the consequences of our words and actions. It is like a law of nature. My wife drilled this concept into our kids. If she said it once she said it a thousand times, "Your actions all have consequences." And, when she said it, the kids knew there was no "eventually" involved.

If you don't want to endure the negative results of poor decisions, think in advance what your actions are likely to produce. What you do and what you say will have lasting impact on others and on yourself.

24

THERE WILL BE CONSEQUENCES

Life is a series of decisions and choices. We are constantly making choices about both significant and insignificant situations. The advice above is a good example of the importance of consequences. Choices shape the course of our lives. Some people learn a great deal from the consequences of their actions and others seem oblivious and never learn anything.

You may hear some people claim that their actions do not have consequences. This is absolutely not true. Consequences are real and can produce both good and bad results. Our goal is to help you make better choices and deal with the consequences.

Physical consequences are a law of nature. If you touch a hot stove you will get burned. If you walk into the street in front of a truck you will be injured. Behaviors have predictable consequences as well. If you cheat and lie, people will stop doing business with you and your reputation will suffer. If you are not dependable, people will learn not to trust you.

We know of a person who had surgery and was told not to walk on his repaired knee. He ignored the doctor's orders and hobbled around on crutches anyway. He lost his balance, fell through a glass door, and received additional injuries. He blamed the doctor for an outcome that was clearly the consequence of his own poor choice.

By definition consequences occur as a result of something else happening. They are the outcome of some other action. The result may occur immediately or it could take a while, even years. This is often one of the reasons that we make poor choices – the consequence does not occur immediately and because of this we think there will never be consequences. We cannot allow this delay to persuade us that consequences don't happen. Living a better life means we are patient and persevere, knowing that what we do matters, regardless of when the result of our actions manifest themselves in real life.

The actual consequences you experience will vary depending on your circumstances, but there will be consequences nonetheless. The degree or size of the consequence will also vary, but we should not be fooled into thinking small transgressions are insignificant. Even seemingly small actions can produce significant consequences.

"One who steals has no right
to complain if he is robbed."
Aesop[4]

THE SLACKER

There was a farmer who had been plowing hard for many days with an ox and mule yoked together. The ox told the mule that they should pretend to be sick and rest. The mule declined saying, "No, we must get the work done, for the season is short." But the ox played sick and the farmer brought him hay and corn and made him comfortable.

When the mule came in from plowing the ox asked how things had gone. The mule said, "We didn't get as much done but we did okay, I guess." The ox asked, "Did the old man say anything about me?" Nothing," said the mule. The next day the ox played sick again. When the tired mule came in he asked again how it went. "All right, but we sure didn't get much done." The ox asked, "What did the old man say about me?" The mule replied, "Nothing directly to me, but he had a long talk with the butcher."[5]

This is similar to the message in the old story concerning the consequences of a hearty breakfast to the chicken and the pig. A breakfast of ham and eggs to the chicken is a temporary inconvenience, but to the pig it is a permanent and lasting consequence – it's a <u>real</u> commitment.

You will need to make a real commitment if you want to guard your speech. You may find it tempting to be lazy, particularly if no one is looking over your shoulder. Sooner or later that behavior will catch up with you.

We chose the word "slacker" as the heading for this story although it is typically not used today. It means someone who avoids his work or obligations. The synonyms for slacker may surprise you: no-account, vagrant, good-for-nothing, and bum. If you tend to get a little lazy with your undertakings, remember the ox in this story. The projected destination for the ox was not a desirable result. You cannot afford to be lazy or apathetic when it comes to how well you are going to live life.

All actions have consequences!

COUNT THE COST

Someone has said that you will ultimately be invited to a party where you will dine on your own consequences. Whether your actions were wise or unwise, you will eventually bear the consequences. Thus, it is important to think about the consequences in advance and count the cost. What will result from your words or actions?

If you don't want to endure the negative results of poor choices, think in advance what your actions are likely to produce. What will you say when co-workers urge you to join them at the local bar every night before you go home? What will you say if someone makes a sexual advance or lurid remark? What will you do or say if you are offered some form of drug? What will you do or say if someone who has been drinking offers you a ride home? What will you do if you are encouraged to cheat or lie?

Regardless of the particular situation, it will always be easier to arrive at a positive outcome if you have thought ahead, evaluated the circumstances, and determined in advance how you will respond to these types of situations.

What you do and say in questionable circumstances will have a lasting impact on your life. This truth is almost as important as understanding that the world is round and not flat. Emblazon the following truth in your mind and on your heart:

Consequences shape lives.
Choices produce consequences
which direct the course of life.
Therefore, count the cost!

ENVY

The Oxford Dictionary describes envy as a feeling of discontented or resentful longing aroused by someone else's possessions, qualities, luck, or situation. Envy is not an attractive attribute. You may think the grass is greener

28

in that other field but it may not be as attractive as you think. Buddha has said:

> **"Do not overrate what you have received,**
> **nor envy others. He who envies others**
> **does not obtain peace of mind."**
> Buddha[6]

There is no purpose or peace in envy. Coveting the things of others, whether they are material objects, mental abilities, or acquired skills, will not produce anything worthwhile. Honoré de Balzac has said, "Envy is the most stupid of vices, for there is no single advantage to be gained from it."[7] He is absolutely right! I challenge you to think of a positive attribute of envy.

Consider the following questions:

- Why do you want it? Is it something you need or simply want?

- Envy implies jealousy, covetousness, and resentment. Which of these is driving your envy?

- If you acquire the object of your envy, what are you going to do with it? Why?

It is certainly appropriate to admire people of character and status. It is also appropriate to desire and copy their good habits and character traits. But that's not envy.

Determine what you want and define your goals in terms of what you want your life to be. Don't waste time resenting or desiring what your neighbor has.

LEGACY

Our words and actions can have impact for a long time. The ongoing impact of poor behavior is a concept that escapes many people. Poor decisions can affect a family for many generations. Bad behavior establishes a pattern that becomes the blueprint for a child's future behavior. For example, parents who frequently lie are modeling lying as an acceptable way to avoid responsibility, inherently teaching their children that lying and deception are acceptable ways of behaving.

What children experience become their normal responses in similar situations. What is witnessed by small children is later reproduced. They can learn to be trustworthy, reliable, and dependable, or they can learn to do drugs, smoke, and gossip. What a child sees modeled in his home becomes his normal response, and that behavior cycle continues into future generations.

> *Your actions, both good and bad, establish the foundation of your life, lifestyle, and legacy.*

Your legacy extends into future generations; therefore, be sure that it is a positive one! Most people have no concept of how their behavior can impact the future. This is dramatically demonstrated by comparing the lives of Jonathan Edwards and Max Jukes.

Jonathan Edwards was a Puritan preacher in the 1700s. His descendants demonstrate the powerful influence of wise choices and a godly life. At the turn of the 20th century, A. E. Winship decided to trace the descendants of Jonathan Edwards and compare them to a man known as Max Jukes.

Mr. Jukes was incarcerated in the New York prison system at the time Jonathan Edwards was preaching. Winship found that 42 of the men in the New York prison system could trace their heritage back to Max Jukes. Jukes, an atheist, lived a godless life. He married an ungodly woman, and from the descendants of this union 310 died as paupers, 150 were criminals, 7 were murderers, and more than half of the women were prostitutes.

In contrast, the record of Jonathan Edwards' progeny tells a much different story. An investigation of 1,394 known descendants of Jonathan Edwards revealed

- 13 college presidents,
- 65 college professors,
- 3 United States Senators,
- 30 judges,
- 100 lawyers,
- 60 physicians,
- 75 army and navy officers,
- 100 preachers and missionaries,
- 60 authors of prominence,
- 1 Vice-President of the United States,
- 80 public officials in other capacities,
- 295 college graduates.

Today, instead of the blessings like those that came to Jonathan Edwards' progeny, we are seeing a growing multitude like the descendants of Max Jukes! Have you seen a family in which the grandfather was an alcoholic – and his sons and grandsons abuse alcohol, too? Have you seen a family plagued with sickness, drug abuse, debt,

31

poverty? Often that is because someone did not make good choices. We are going to leave a legacy for our children and grandchildren. Will we pass on a blessing or a curse?[8]

If you want to leave a legacy,
impact someone's life.

WE REAP WHAT WE SOW

In a number of proverbs, King Solomon suggests that right living is to be preferred over wickedness. He describes the nature of righteousness as being immovable and that it will stand above the wicked. The wicked, on the other hand, are not secure and will ultimately perish.[9]

Is your desire for right living rooted deeply or is it planted in shallow sandy soil that can easily be washed away? Solomon indicated that the wicked would ultimately be overthrown and perish and that the righteous would survive because their character had a root that is deep and impossible to dislodge.

Solomon tells us that our decisions matter and it is better to be on the side of the righteous than to take up with the wicked. The reasoning is the same as the man who builds his house on rock or sand. If we build on sand (evil or foolish ways) then our hopes and plans will never stand up against the storms of life. If we build on rock (honesty, wisdom) our plans will hold firm.

We will reap what we sow and if we sow badly because we have rejected or ignored what is right, the wise counsel of

SPEECH LIFE PRINCIPLE: Guard your speech.

friends, or our own core values, we will reap the consequences. Those who think they know everything reject the wisdom of the wise and follow their own plans and schemes. It can be said that those who insist on following their own ways will end up choking on them.

**Since we reap what we sow,
build your life on truth, integrity, and good will.**

Lysa Terkeurst in her book, *The Best Yes* says, this about making decisions: "The decision you make determines the schedule you keep. The schedule you keep determines the life you live. And how you live your life determines how you spend your soul."

Think about that statement. You could say this truth in a number of ways – Ms. Terkeurst chose this particular description. But any way you say it the meaning is, *your decisions determine your life*. The consequences of your decisions constitute your day and your future. You are always living in the midst of the choices you make, therefore, make good choices. The consequences will determine how you live your life, or in Terkeurst's words, how you "spend your soul."

IT'S NOT FAIR

Unfortunately, life is not fair. Worrying about fairness, arguing about it, or fighting it will be of little value. Being "fair" generally means that everyone is treated equally (the concept of socialism). The issue of something being fair often tends to become more important to us when it impacts us personally. When something touches us directly, we become concerned about fairness.

But life is not fair!

If you believe that life is intended to be fair, then it's not fair to others less fortunate that you were born in America and are therefore privileged. It is not fair that you have avoided poverty, wars, terrorism, natural disasters, tyrants, dying in an accident, abuse . . .

Obviously it is unrealistic to argue it's not fair that we experience the consequences of our own poor choices, especially since we are the ones making those poor choices. If we think we shouldn't incur the result of our poor choices then we certainly should not expect to experience the rewards of our good choices. We must accept the fact that life is not necessarily fair and that "bad things do happen to good people."

Obviously, things happen to us that are completely random or out of our control. We can't control weather disasters, traffic accidents, or illness. We can reduce the chances of those problems by taking precautions when bad weather threatens, by driving carefully, and by making heathy choices. But we can't eliminate them all. In the end, we control what we can by making good choices and understand that some things in life simply are not fair.

Think about the consequences,
then choose wisely!

WHO TO BLAME

Blame is a big concern for many people today. When something bad happens, the first reaction by many is to find someone to blame. Many people no longer accept the concept of an "accident." It's become the norm to assign blame and "make someone pay." We have forgotten the definition of an accident: an unplanned or unforeseen occurrence. It is no longer acceptable to merely restore the victim to their position before an accident. Rather we think we must extract a huge monetary punishment from the other party.

Some of us react in illogical ways to consequences. The most illogical is the person who totally ignores the obvious dangers of what they are about to do and then rather than accepting the consequences, casts blame. They become angry or embarrassed and attempt to find someone or something to blame in order to take the attention off their own poor judgment.

Taking responsibility for mistakes, misunderstandings, or accidents is becoming a lost art because many children have been raised to believe they do not have to suffer consequences. If the result of some action is not good or right, they expect someone else will fix it and the boss, parent, or coach has no right to hold them responsible.

Admitting mistakes and taking responsibility is a characteristic of those who are living their best life.

MISTAKES!

What happens when we make a mistake? A mistake is not the end of the world – it's a mistake, not a death sentence! If we make a wrong choice, we must rethink the issue and select another path. We all make mistakes. The real challenge in life is how we handle those mistakes.

Statistics say that successful entrepreneurs on the average have seven failed business ventures before they finally succeed. What does this tell us? If something is not working or the desired result is not occurring, stop and change direction. Try something new.

Not every choice we make will be the right decision. Expect some failures in life and don't be overwhelmed if what you choose does not work out as you expect. If the choice was bad, wrong, or ill-advised, fix it!

Pride will often cause us to hide mistakes.

TIPS TO AVOID UNINTENDED CONSEQUENCES

No one intentionally makes bad choices. We may make poor choices simply because we did not understand the consequences. In reality, however, we may be overlooking the consequences because we want to follow a certain course of action.

Regardless of the reason, unintended or poor results sometimes occur. However, there are ways we can reduce the probability of negative results and increase the probability of positive results. Here are five tips you could adopt before making decisions:

1. LOOK (THINK) before you leap!

> Take time to consider the consequences.
> Ask yourself, "What would 'wisdom' do?"
> Think logically.

2. LISTEN to the advice of others.

> Seek out trusted friends.
> But, remember, others have their own agendas.

3. CONSIDER the pros and cons.

> How will this decision impact me or others?
> Will I be proud of the outcome?
> What would my mother think?

4. BE PATIENT.

> "Sleep on it" is often excellent advice.
> Research as much as you can.

5. EMOTIONS often cause poor decisions.

> Base your choices on facts and reality.
> Do not make decisions based on your emotions.
> Emotions can have disastrous impact on decisions.

TIPS I COULD USE

a. Underline, circle, or highlight the 1 to 3 tips above that you think could make the most impact if you implemented them in your life. You will revisit these choices at the end of the book in the Planning section.

b. There may be other things that you think would make a difference. Write them below:

_____

_____

_____

_____

It is the peculiar quality of a fool to perceive the faults of others and to forget his own.

Cicero[10]

Chapter 3

SPEECH LIFE PRINCIPLE

Guard Your Speech

*"Communication is a skill that you can learn.
It's like riding a bicycle or typing.
If you're willing to work at it, you can rapidly
improve the quality of every part of your life."*
Brian Tracy[11]

Our personal character, traits, and habits are the foundation of who we are. These attributes determine what we say and what we do. Our character reflects what we really believe and what we value. If we have the inherent desire to do what is right, we will likely have a high regard for our words and how our speech impacts those around us. If our sense of right and wrong is blurred, then our adherence to speech that produces harmony and agreement may also be blurred.

39

This book focuses on our speech: what we say and what we imply with the words we use. Our personal character will influence our speech: reasonable and uplifting words versus crusty abusive speech. The resulting speech will often determine our ability to live a successful life.

What we say and how we say it are influenced a great deal by our ability to control our feelings and emotions which can cause us to speak when it would have been prudent to remain silent. Our Life Planning Series will include separate books on related subjects like anger, patience, temptation, and life balance under the category of "Self-Control." These additional books may be helpful to you.

> *"The mouth is the portal of the mind. If not carefully guarded, it leaks true intents and motives. Feelings are the feet of the mind. If not carefully watched, they will take you onto all kinds of wayward paths."*
> Hong Zicheng[12]

Following are four examples that demonstrate the importance of what we say:

1. A person of high character says the same thing in private as when people are listening.

2. People of lesser character think it is acceptable to say anything as long as it benefits their own personal agenda.

3. History and experience demonstrate that poorly chosen words can be hurtful, misleading, and even incendiary.

4. Reputations can be damaged beyond repair by a few poorly chosen words.

There is an old Chinese proverb that says, "If you wish to know the mind of a man, listen to his words."[13] Our true character is revealed in our words because out of the overflow of our words, the heart speaks. How you think, what you believe, and your true character are revealed by your words.

We believe that high character is one of the fundamental characteristics of one who desires to live a successful life. Our speech and what we imply with our words is a foundational trait underlying our character. Thus, this subject is one of the five Primary Life Principles:

SPEECH LIFE PRINCIPLE:

Guard Your Speech.

If you adopt this Primary Life Principle for your life, you can make great strides toward living a life of satisfaction and peace. Guarding the words you speak is a gateway to that life. You will never be able to be all you can be if loose speech and careless words are a part of your character and ongoing lifestyle.

"Words are singularly the most powerful force available to humanity. We can choose to use this force constructively with words of encouragement, or destructively using words of despair. Words have energy and power with the ability to help, to heal, to hinder, to hurt, to harm, to humiliate and to humble."
Yehuda Berg[14]

This quote describes our speech as "the most powerful force available to humanity." That is a very strong statement regarding the power of our words, but it is true. Our words can devastate or heal. They can spread peace, love, or hatred. They can start or end conflict between family members, friends, strangers, or even nations.

In this day and age, words spoken in one place can literally be heard or viewed around the world in seconds. The power of the word, whether spoken or written, can scarcely be understated.

> **"Words have no wings**
> **but they can fly a thousand miles."**
> Korean Proverb[15]

Therefore, guarding your speech and choosing your words carefully is of prime importance. If one is not careful with words, it will be very difficult to have a life that is in balance. The scars of a life built on the turmoil and chaos generated by rough, harsh, and demanding speech will be a difficult path.

If you choose gentle, caring, and intelligent speech, life will be much smoother. You will inherently receive the benefit of kind words and loving concern from those around you. Guarding your speech will produce harmony, agreement, compromise, and even laughter.

Make it a primary life goal to guard your speech
and uplift others with your words.

Chapter 4

Choose Your Words Carefully

"The one who guards his mouth protects his life;
the one who opens his lips invites his own ruin."
Proverbs 13:3[16]

"Words spoken can never be recalled."
Wentworth Dillon[17]

"If you can't say anything nice,
then don't say anything at all."
Aesop[18]

THE DAMAGE HAS BEEN DONE

A man once said something about his neighbor that was untrue. The word spread around the small town very quickly. But soon the truth came out—what could the man do? He went to see the local priest and the priest gave him some strange instructions. "Take a bag full of feathers and place one feather on the doorstep of each person who heard the untrue story you told. Then go back a day later, pick up the feather, and bring the bag back to me." So the man did as the priest said. But when he went back to pick up the feathers nearly all of them were gone. When he went back to the priest he said, "Father, I did as you said

43

but when I went back the wind had blown the feathers away and I could not get them back." And the priest replied, "So it is with careless words, my son. Once they are spoken, they cannot be taken back. You may ask for forgiveness for what you said but you cannot take your words back. The damage has already been done."[19]

I don't know if this story actually occurred, but I do know that the lesson it teaches is absolutely true. It's like sending an email that you wish you had not sent. Once it's gone you cannot stop it. You will be stuck with the consequences of what you said.

Given the underlying truth of this story, it is critical that we are very conscious of what we say because as this example illustrates, words cannot be unsaid. We can always apologize for foolish words, try to make amends, but we are in a deep hole that will not be easy to fill. Benjamin Franklin said, *"The heart of a fool is in his mouth, but the mouth of a wise man is in his heart."*[20]

What does this mean? In general, it means that a fool is absurd and will reason wrongly. Thus, a fool will make wrong decisions and then take wrong actions. Franklin indicated that the source of the fool's behavior was his mouth. What the fool says proves he is a fool. But Franklin said that the wise man speaks from his heart, meaning his inner source of knowledge and understanding. The wise man will have wisdom from his inner being to call on before he speaks.

CHOOSE WORDS CAREFULLY

Much of what people say has very little meaning or importance. Some just talk to hear the sound of their

44

voice. Most of us need to be more aware of our speech and the impact our words have on others. Words can do great damage and those who speak carelessly can find themselves suffering unpleasant consequences.

Our speech should always be kind and gracious. Gracious speech is polite and shows respect to the one we are talking to. It is pleasing and acceptable, not grating, harsh, or inappropriate.

In addition, our speech lasts for a period of time. It does not just dissipate never to be seen or heard again. It's likely to endure for an extended period of time. Thus, we need to be sure what we are saying will stand the test of time, and be appropriate no matter when the words are heard or seen.

Sometimes we must be able to quickly think on our feet in to order to answer questions, respond to a situation, or to say positive things about other people. The story is told about a seven-foot-tall man who walked up to the counter at McDonalds, slammed down his big fist and said to the girl behind the counter, "I want half a Big Mac." She said, "What?" He said again, "I want half a Big Mac and I want it now!" Not being sure what to do, she said, "Excuse me for a minute." And she headed back to her manager without realizing that the man was following right behind her.

She got back to the manager and said, "There's a big klutz out there who is dumber than lead and he has ordered half a Big Mac." And just then she suddenly realized the man was standing right behind her. She quickly added: "And this gentleman wants the other half."[21]

Have you ever caught yourself just in the nick of time? I usually catch myself just _after_ the nick of time. I have a tendency to speak without thinking of the impact of my words. The girl behind the counter in this story was a quick-thinker. Unfortunately, we are not all gifted with this ability so our speech may tend to get us into trouble at times. Sometimes it is easy to maneuver around our inappropriate words, but other times it can result in a painful situation.

THINK BEFORE YOU SPEAK

We must be aware of what we are saying and think before we speak. Many who have spoken too soon have regretted their quick responses. Speaking without thinking can result in embarrassment and being considered foolish.

Those who speak quickly and without forethought can find themselves in the same situation as the fool who speaks without knowledge. This is a serious warning to those who think they must be the first to speak. There are a number of dangers in speaking too quickly, Here are four:

- Our quick reaction is often not on target with what is being discussed.

- The result is embarrassment because of ill-advised words that would have been better unsaid.

- There is a danger that we appear to be speaking of something we know little or nothing about.

- Butting into someone else's conversation can result in becoming a target, rather than a participant in the discussion.

Taking time to think about what you will say may also cause others to think you are wise. Obviously you want to have something worthwhile to contribute, and pausing to speak can give you time to consider your response. You never want to say something hurtful. Your comments should be helpful, useful, and appropriate.

It is always good to consider if what you are saying is adding to the conversation. Ask yourself if what you are about to say is worthwhile and not some meaningless comment that makes it appear you want attention.

Here are some basic questions you could ask yourself:

- Have I listened long enough that I understand the discussion?

- Is what I have to say a repeat of what others have already said?

- Will what I have to say add to the conversation?

- Is it worth saying?

Do not under any circumstances lie or embellish what you are saying. Lies and dishonesty can destroy your character faster than you can offer an apology.

If you are going to make a comment about another person, choose your words carefully. Think about whether your comments are something that needs to be said. Is it absolutely true? Is it kind? Why are you choosing to make these comments? What are your motives?

You might ask yourself if what you are about to say is meaningful or useful. Even if your words are true, does revealing this information accomplish any good purpose? Think before you speak and make sure that what you have to say is helpful and part of a solution and not part of the problem.

There is usually no good purpose talking about others, particularly if you hurt or belittle someone. If you frequently attempt to put others in a bad light, your friends will begin to suspect that you also talk about them when they are not around. Be very cautious of what you say about others!

There are many proverbial sayings that imply it is wise to remain silent rather than to speak. Speaking too quickly or about something you have limited knowledge about can often result in embarrassing situations. If you continually make noise with your mouth and say nothing of value, people will tend to ignore you when you are speaking. People will listen if you have the reputation of speaking intelligently. If you are speaking simply to be the center of attention, you probably have nothing worthwhile to contribute.

"You have it easily in your power to increase the sum total of this world's happiness now. How?
By giving a few words of sincere appreciation
to someone who is lonely or discouraged.
Perhaps you will forget tomorrow the kind words
you say today, but the recipient may
cherish them over a lifetime."
Dale Carnegie[22]

HARSH VERSUS GENTLE WORDS

The problem with harsh words is that someone often gets hurt. Harsh talk hastens destruction and increases the pace of an eroding situation. People can be hurt, embarrassed, or even ruined by harsh speech.

Conversely it is often said that gentle speech will calm a situation and protect one from negative consequences.

The saying that, "a gentle answer turns away anger," sounds simplistic but it is true. It is difficult to pick a fight with a quiet, calm, and gentle person. Someone who responds with a gentle answer is normally not perceived to be a threat. It is common sense that harsh words will stir up wrath, anger, retribution, fury, or outrage. The fool will often blurt out harsh words that can break the spirit (crush one mentally or emotionally).

In contrast to harsh or angry words, a gentle answer is far more attractive and appealing. An answer given calmly, without loud demonstration, with knowledge and wisdom, will normally produce a positive result. Have you ever witnessed a gentle answer or soft-spoken word taking the air out of an argument? It's very difficult for a person to remain aggressive, angry, or pushy when the other party is not reacting to their bluster.

However, in some cases, a quiet gentle response can be viewed as weak. The quiet person may not be taken seriously. Therefore, even though our speech is gentle, it must carry authority and conviction. Gentle speech should not be perceived as being weak, but rather demonstrate a rock solid core that is based on knowledge and conviction.

Someone who has been offended can be difficult to talk to. Barriers can be created in a conversation by poorly chosen words causing effective communication to be difficult after that has happened. The person who is insulted, put down, or made to appear foolish will be hard to engage in useful conversation. An insult can be difficult to overcome because they are no longer engaged. They are either hurt and want to leave or are thinking about what they could say to disarm or silence the offender.

FIVE TIPS FOR CHOOSING WORDS WISELY

1. Think about what you are saying.

Do you know the meaning of the words you are using? Are your words sending the right message or can they be misunderstood or misinterpreted? Do you know how others will react when they hear or read your words? What is a likely response to what you are about to say?

2. Do not make insincere promises.

Do you say you will do something or that you will do your best when you have no intention of doing anything? Don't say you will "give it your best shot" if you intend to ignore the situation. We need to make our "trying" real in order not to give others false hope. If you are not sure you can do something, be truthful about it. Don't allow insincere promises or vague responses damage your reputation.

Make all shoulds, woulds, and coulds, into "I will" promises. Shoulda, woulda, and coulda are for those who have no intention of doing anything. If you can't or don't want to do something, be truthful with those wanting a commitment. If you know you should, then do it and feel good about doing it. The truth is far better than leaving people hanging when you bail on a promise because you were embarrassed to say "No."

3. Be clear and positive.

Hoping something will happen is not very reassuring. When you say you will do something, make sure your words are understood. Be clear about what you say you are going to do and not do. Don't allow your communication to be so complex or convoluted that others are confused.

4. Don't make statements or commitments based on future probabilities.

Don't make promises based on something else happening or on someone else fulfilling their promise. You have no control over the future or the actions of others. Don't put yourself at the mercy of conditions over which you have no control.

5. Sometimes you must say "No," or "I can't."

There are many things we cannot do and it is acceptable to say you can't when either time or abilities do not allow you to do something. Just be sure you don't use "can't" as a way to avoid responsibilities.

TIPS YOU COULD USE

a. Underline, circle, or highlight the 1 to 3 tips above that you think could make the most impact if you implemented them in your life. You will revisit these choices at the end of the book in the Planning section.

b. There may be other things that you think would make a difference. Write them below:

_____

_____

_____

_____

Chapter 5

Gossip

"People gossip. People are insecure, so they talk about other people so that they won't be talked about. They point out flaws in other people to make them feel good about themselves."
Blake Lively[23]

DO NOT GOSSIP

Most people will respond to the admonition not to gossip by saying, "I never gossip! This certainly does not apply to me! It's someone else's character deficiency, not mine." Really! Are you sure? Webster defines a gossip as someone who habitually reveals personal or sensational information about someone else. I suspect that the only exception for some of us is that the definition says it's habitual.

Words that spread gossip and slander are particularly offensive. A slanderer is one who is a liar and who causes trouble for others. Their words are often slanted to make themselves look good. But, lies typically come home to roost. The one spreading slander eventually will be found out and will usually suffer the consequences.

Gossip and malicious talk can end friendships, put off acquaintances, and separate one from a group. Gossip, even if true, can end any hope of a relationship because trust is lost. If the gossip is malicious or destructive the situation can be even worse.

> **"Isn't it kind of silly to think that tearing someone else down builds you up?"**
> Sean Covey[24]

Those who listen to gossip are often as guilty as the one speaking the words. If no one listens, the person spreading the gossip has no one to talk to. Gossip should not be encouraged or condoned. Good people should put a stop to it when it begins.

What do you do if you find yourself in a conversation that involves gossip? One solution is simply to excuse yourself and leave. If you feel brave, you can challenge the gossipers by stating that you do not condone gossip and will leave if the conversation cannot move on to something worthwhile. Unfortunately, many of us remain in the conversation and say nothing. But by being a quiet bystander, we are participating and inherently approving the conversation!

Have you ever told someone a secret and then learned they did not keep it confidential? You can imagine how people feel who are on the receiving end of such betrayal. Having a continuing relationship with the betrayer is extremely difficult. It is very hard to work or associate with that person until the situation is resolved. Obviously you would be unwise to share any type of confidential information with that person in the future.

If you are ever tempted to gossip, consider these questions:

- Would I share this information about myself?

- Am I breaking a confidence?

- What are my motives? Why am I sharing this information?

- Will someone be hurt?

- Am I willing to be identified as the source?

"No one gossips about
other people's secret virtues."
Bertrand Russell[25]

DANGERS OF GOSSIP

Why do people gossip? Obviously gossip can be used intentionally to ruin the reputation of another. But it is often to make the teller seem important to those hearing the information. Having information that others do not have can make some people feel important. Others may think you are one of the people "in the know."

Gossip can become addictive because it draws attention to the one passing on information. Other people can be drawn into a group because interesting or private information is being shared. The problem is that the person being discussed has no one to defend them. There is no way to confirm the truth of what is being said.

In order to stop the gossip, it is usually necessary for someone to take a stand and say they are uncomfortable discussing private information that cannot be confirmed. Beginning a new subject or leaving the group may be the only reasonable options.

"Gossiping and lying go hand in hand."
(Unknown)

RELATIONSHIPS:
Gossip can destroy friendships as well as casual relationships. If someone speaks about someone else, that discussion often gets back to the one being discussed. The result is generally embarrassing for the participants. When someone talks about another, whether true or untrue, private or public, it always damages a relationship.

Friends simply do not share personal information about other friends. Serious relationship problems occur when the information shared was confidential or not appropriate for sharing with others.

TRUST:
A friend does not expect to hear anything (confidential or not) from others that was spoken to another friend. Friendships are built on trust and idle words and gossip can destroy a relationship.

RUMORS:
Gossip or idle chatter about others can spread lies and untruths very easily. Innocent comments can be misunderstood or intentionally misinterpreted. Never pass along rumors.

REPUTATIONS:
Gossip is often spread by those who desire power over others. Gossip can quickly ruin good reputations. A reputation takes years to establish but it can be destroyed in days. Trying to rebuild a reputation ruined by gossip can be very difficult, if not impossible.

> **"The things most people want to know about are usually none of their business."**
> George Bernard Shaw[26]

JUDGING PEOPLE BASED ON GOSSIP
Don't judge people based on gossip. You have no idea what is true and what is false. Your best course of action is to base your opinion of people on your own personal experience and not change that opinion unless you have personal knowledge or experience about a situation

YOU MAY BE NEXT
If you know people who gossip, stay away from them. You certainly don't want them as friends and there is normally no good reason to associate with them. If you associate with gossips, others will assume that you also gossip.

Be extremely careful about what you say to a gossip. Innocent comments can be twisted and made to put you in a questionable situation.

> *"Whoever gossips to you, will gossip about you."*
> Spanish Proverb[27]

WORDS CAN HURT

An old saying declares that sticks and stones can do damage but words cannot hurt you. That's rubbish! Words can be extremely hurtful. They can destroy relationships. They can cause depression, anger, and hurt feelings.

SUMMARY

The bottom line about gossip is, "Tight lips don't sink ships." If you guard your words they will not cause harm. If you tend to be loose with information about others, tighten up your speech and pass along compliments rather than gossip. If you are in the presence of people gossiping, tell them you will not participate in such a conversation and move on if they persist.

Gossip can steal your joy or the joy of others.

Put an end to gossip!

> *"Gossip needn't be false to be evil – there's a lot of truth that shouldn't be passed around."*
> *Frank A. Clark[28]*

RESULTS OF GOSSIP - SUMMARY

1. You Lose Trust

Nobody likes or trusts a gossip.

2. You May Be Spreading Lies

If you are repeating gossip you have no way to know whether it is true. If you pass on information obtained from gossip there is a very high probability that you are spreading lies about someone. Such lies can be very damaging because it is very difficult to stop the spread or correct the information.

Make sure you know the difference between repeating information and spreading gossip. If you have not been able to verify the information you are sharing, it should be left unsaid. Don't spread gossip out of revenge or frustration.

3. Gossip Can Come Back to Haunt You

If you talk about others, others will often talk about you. What you have to say about others, both good and bad, will be known by those whom you discuss. So, if you don't want the problems associated with being "the person with the big mouth," it's wise to consider what you have to say before you say it. Don't say anything about other people that you would object to if it was said about you.

4. Keep Secrets

In close friendships, confidences are often shared. Always think of personal information as private and never repeat it. Don't try to be the center of attention by telling secrets or repeating what you learned in private conversations with others. If you promise not to share information, be sure to keep that promise!

Never break a confidence!

5. Gossip Will Isolate You

If you gossip or even just repeat information about others, you soon will have a reputation as a gossip. Others will be very careful around you because they know you will tell others what was said and what was done. You will find this a very effective way to lose friends!

6. Gossip Impacts Your Reputation

If you gain a reputation as a gossip, you will not only lose trust with friends and associates, but it will probably impact other personal character traits. Your integrity will come under question. You will lose respect. People will doubt your sincerity.

7. Negative Impact on Others

One of the very serious consequences of gossip is that other people will be hurt. Those people impacted by gossip will often be damaged or even disgraced. They will also be frustrated because it is very difficult to correct the misinformation and the resulting damage.

"Great minds discuss ideas.
Average minds discuss events.
Small minds discuss people."
Eleanor Roosevelt[29]

ONE LAST WORD

One last word of warning: those who habitually gossip are always in danger of slipping over the line into slander. What's the difference? Gossip occurs when people talk about other people. What gossips spread may or may not be true. Often it has a grain of truth but may be embellished. Slander, however, is the act of repeating or spreading malicious lies about someone with the intent of harming their reputation.

The biggest difference is that gossip is essentially a social issue. Along with libel (a published false statement that is damaging to a person's reputation), slander is a legal issue. A person can be sued for either slander or libel. The point here is that those who routinely gossip put themselves in the precarious position of edging over into slander or libel. It's obviously better not to put oneself at risk by avoiding gossip entirely.

TIPS: HOW TO CONTROL GOSSIP

1. Don't talk about others – hold your tongue.

Don't participate in gossip under any circumstances.

2. Avoid participation in groups talking about others.

If the group continues talking about people, excuse yourself and leave. If you are concerned about how others will feel about your leaving, know that at least some will respect your courage and commitment.

3. Call out individuals who continue to gossip.

In some instances you may be forced to call a gossip, a gossip. You must do this gently and with loving intent.

4. Convince gossips that their speech can reap undesirable consequences.

5. Drop gossips as friends or associates.

> *"Speaking your truth with love assures that others will hear your message, since angry words can shut down communications."*
> Doreen Virtue[30]

TIPS YOU COULD USE

a. Underline, circle, or highlight the 1 to 5 tips or suggestions in this chapter that might make the most impact if you implemented it in your life. You will revisit these choices at the end of the book in the Planning section.

b. There may be other things that you think would make a
difference. Write them below:

_____

_____

_____

_____

_____

_____

Chapter 6

Gloating, Boasting, and Bragging

"Wise men speak because they have something to say;
Fools because they have to say something."
Plato[31]

Speech and words can be misused in many ways. For example we can boast, gloat, gossip, and brag about any number of things. It is preferable to speak with grace. We must continually be aware of the impact of our speech. We should ask ourselves, "What will my words mean to others?" Our speech should be guarded and flavored with positive messages that support and build up our friends, family, and associates.

DO NOT GLOAT

The Oxford Languages Dictionary defines the word gloat as "to contemplate or dwell on one's own success or another's misfortune with smugness or malignant pleasure." We probably all know people who act like this and such people are often not well liked because they take pleasure in the failures or losses of others.

There is only temporary joy in gloating!

I have a friend whose daughter was engaged to the son of a very "upper crust" family. The father of the groom, Mr. Wonderful, held a very prestigious job and Mrs. Wonderful was an immaculate homemaker and did not have to work at an outside job. My friend and his wife were constantly hearing about Mr. and Mrs. Wonderful and how they could do no wrong. On the other hand my friends were on the receiving end of put-downs and seemingly did everything wrong.

The wedding rehearsal dinner, arranged by Mr. and Mrs. Wonderful, was to be catered by a local establishment with a highly recognized chef. However, on that night the caterers did not show up and there was no food. Apparently Mrs. Wonderful failed to confirm her reservation so the chef assumed the dinner was off. Oops! The Wonderfuls were in shock and paralyzed from the neck down.

So the father of the bride (my friend) stepped in, made a couple of phone calls and in 30 minutes had reservations at a very nice restaurant in town. All the guests had to move to the new location but nothing was ever said as to why the move had to take place.

The bride and her parents had reason to gloat but nothing was ever said. Would you have remained silent? Was silence the best response? If this was your daughter's in-laws, what would you advise?

Most of us can understand that gloating over our successes or the failure of others is not a very attractive attribute. It will do nothing to win friends or influence enemies. One who suffers may deserve bad fortune, but we should not take pleasure in that suffering.

Observers generally know when someone displays fake humility. Likewise they will see through gloating. Does gloating ever have a good purpose? No, even if the suffering is deserved.

DON'T BOAST OR BRAG

Someone who boasts expresses excessive pride in something he has done. Boasting results from pride or conceit and is accompanied by an inordinate amount of self-esteem. Pride is all about self and not about anyone else. The boaster becomes wrapped up in himself and his own self-importance. He becomes smug and pompous.

Boasting is often an attempt to put ourselves in the spotlight. That is not an attractive behavior. Most people boast because they want to bring attention to themselves.

People who do good works or say kind things get attention for a job well done without the need to brag about themselves. It is always best if the praise comes from others. If our bragging stretches the truth about our abilities, we can end up looking even more like a fool when the truth is revealed.

Does that mean we cannot take credit for a good job? No. Boasting is taking undue credit for some accomplishment. When a person receives credit from another for a job well done an appropriate response is, "Thank you very much. I had a lot of help from . . ."

Guard your words.

BRAGGING: TIPS

Bragging is annoying to those in the audience. Nobody wants to hear how great you are. If you have accomplished something important, your actions and the results speak for themselves. You can certainly be proud of the things you have accomplished, but don't bore or irritate others by bragging about them. Let others boast about what you have done if they think it is worth repeating.

Here are some tips to keep boasting or bragging under control:

1. Rather than bragging about your own accomplishments, brag about your co-workers or your employees. Boasting about others, whether related to work, family, church, or community services is much more attractive. Just be sure to stick to the facts and talk about your appreciation for the accomplishment or the help you received. It is not necessary to talk about specifics.

2. When you are speaking of accomplishments, use common sense. Don't compare yourself to others in a manner that would irritate or provoke your coworkers.

When you speak about others always say positive things. Do not criticize co-workers in public or private.

3. Don't take credit for something you did not do.

4. Whenever you talk about yourself, be humble.

5. Never compare yourself to other people. In any comparison one of the choices is better than another. The person who is being outperformed will not appreciate your comments, even if true. Such discussion should occur only in private.

6. Know the audience! Be aware of who will hear or read your words. Be careful not to offend or anger someone because you failed to consider your listener's feelings or perspectives about the accomplishments you are describing.

7. Be very cautious of what you post on social media about others. Ask permission before you post information about other people. Even positive comments should be cleared with others before you make public statements.

8. Always give credit to others who helped you, regardless of the significance of their contribution.

9. Never talk about your wealth, your possessions, or your income. This subject is never what others want to hear.

10. Don't play the victim and complain about hard work, or that you are exhausted from completing a project. This may sound like you were the only one working hard. Don't wear "Exhausted Worker" as a badge of honor.

11. Don't talk about how busy you are. Everyone is busy and if you talk about your schedule as if it is something special, others will lose interest in what you have to say.

12. Avoid talking about sensitive, delicate, personal, or private subjects related to your work and coworkers. This often appears like you are trying to elevate yourself above your coworkers.

13. If you must speak about your work, talk about the work accomplished rather than your contribution.

14. Model kindness, grace, and forgiveness.

TIPS YOU COULD USE

a. Underline, circle, or highlight the 1 to 3 tips above that you think could make the most impact if you implemented them in your life. You will revisit these choices at the end of the book in the Planning section.

b. There may be other things that you think would make a difference. Write them below:

_____

_____

_____

_____

"Good words are worth much and cost little."
George Herbert[32]

Chapter 7

Be Slow To Speak

"We are masters of the unsaid words,
but slaves of those we let slip out."
Winston Churchill[33]

"The best time for you to hold your tongue
is the time you feel you must say something or bust."
Josh Billings[34]

BE SLOW TO SPEAK

Jean De La Bruyere has said, "We rarely repent of speaking little, but often of speaking too much."[35] There are many proverbs from all over the world that indicate we are wise when we guard our words and think before we speak. The general reason for these wise sayings is that we have a tendency to say too much, speak without thinking, embellish our conversation, and say things we don't really mean.

If you are slow to speak, the implication is that you have listened to what others have said, your response is appropriate, and your words add to the conversation rather than detract. An old proverb states that it is better to remain silent and have people think you're a fool than to open your mouth and remove all doubt!

Foolish speech cannot be taken back or erased. Thus, wise people choose their words carefully and know what they are speaking about. Many a man keeps himself out of trouble by remaining silent.

Remaining silent does not mean you are not part of the conversation. Listening carefully will serve you well. If your comments are always on target, others will notice and be particularly attentive when you speak. Comments that are not directed at the given subject can be very irritating to those engaged in the conversation.

Unless you are the one starting the conversation, it is always smart to take a reading on the discussion before you add your thoughts. There is no advantage to speaking up first or immediately. However, there are advantages of waiting to speak:

- You appear to be wise and discerning, rather than foolish.

- You protect yourself from embarrassment.

- Your contribution is more likely to be a useful addition to the conversation and be recognized for its insight.

Considering what you will say before you speak is logical. You are less likely to be wrong and demonstrate your ignorance or foolishness. A well-thought-out response is likely to be recognized as sound advice. An answer or comment based on considered thought will not be an emotional reaction but information that can improve or advance the conversation.

"Silence is the hardest argument to refute."
(Unknown)

LISTENING

Listening means paying attention to someone in order to understand what they are saying and meaning. Listening involves thoughtful attention. This results in being able to respond to the questions or issues being discussed and not simply speaking about something on one's own personal agenda.

When is listening particularly important?

- When you are engaged in an important conversation.

- When you are receiving instructions.

- When you are being warned about danger.

- When you are being given answers to your questions.

- When you are being asked questions.

The advantage of listening well is that the result of your participation is highly considered. You are not surprised by something that is said because you missed an important point. Attentive listening means that you are alert to what others are saying and implying. You are aware of the implications and you can integrate yourself into the existing discussion smoothly. Listening well means you can speak successfully and effectively on the issues being discussed. You are not changing the subject or redirecting the focus to your own pet subjects.

> *"Think twice before you speak, because your words*
> *and influence will plant the seed of either success*
> *or failure in the mind of another."*
> Napoleon Hill[36]

People who do not listen well will often get into trouble with what they say, be embarrassed because they are off track, or even get ridiculed for their comments. Those who do not listen well often create problems because they respond incorrectly or fail to do what was asked. Poor listeners often suffer the consequences of bad decisions. Their poor response is often because they were not paying attention. They did not do what was asked or respond appropriately.

It is not that difficult to listen if you are intentional about it. Here are a few tips that will help:

- Don't judge others in your conversation.

- Allow others to finish. Don't interrupt.

- Respond to what is being said by others. Don't change the subject.

- Ask good questions. Clarify things you might not understand correctly.

- Don't try to outdo others with your "better" story or illustration.

> *"It takes patience to listen . . . It takes real skill*
> *to pretend that you are actually listening."*
> Nikhil Saluja[37]

Another very important habit is to limit your words. Say what is important and then allow someone else to speak. It is very easy, after we have said what's important, to ramble on because we have this need to make sure everyone understands, or, we just don't know how or when to stop.

In some cases we like to be the center of attention and when we are speaking the attention is on us. Unfortunately, that attention will not last long if what we are saying is a waste of time and not really pertinent to the question or issue at hand.

Think of the conversation as creating a cloud of fog. Are your words adding to the fog or clearing the fog away so that you and others can see clearly? That should be your objective when you speak. Limit your speech and social media comments to what's really important and what will edify your listeners.

Say what's important, then stop speaking!

TIPS YOU COULD USE

a. Underline, circle, or highlight the 1 to 3 tips above that you think could make the most impact if you implemented them in your life. You will revisit these choices at the end of the book in the Planning section.

b. There may be other things that you think would make a difference. Write them below:

_____

_____

_____

_____

Chapter 8

Arguing

*"Nobody is perfect, and nobody deserves to be perfect.
Nobody has it easy, everybody has issues.
You never know what people are going through.
So, pause before you start judging, criticizing, or mocking
others. Everybody is fighting their own unique war."*[38]

DON'T ARGUE OR QUARREL

Let's begin with some definitions. (Oxford University Press)

Discuss – Talk about something so as to reach a decision.
Argue – Exchange diverging or opposite views heatedly.
Quarrel – An angry argument or disagreement.
Conflict – A serious disagreement or argument . . . .
        an incompatibility between opinions, principles, etc.
Quarrelsome – Given to or characterized by quarreling.

Whenever two people are together, the possibility of
differences of opinion exists. In fact, it would be fair to say
differences are inevitable! And when more than two
people are involved, the number of differences increases

dramatically. After all, we're all very different personalities, have different experiences, different beliefs, different interests, and different passions. Life would be very boring if this were not true. The challenge is to coexist with all these differences in peace, harmony, and friendship. How can we maintain a friendship with someone with whom we disagree? Can we argue with someone and remain friends? Is there such a thing as "recreational arguing"? If it exists, is it a positive or negative thing?

The word "discuss" carries no negative connotations. It's simply talking about an issue, with the intent of reaching a decision or consensus on a topic. In business, if several alternatives are presented, a discussion would be held in order to reach agreement on the best option.

The definition for "argue" adds a qualifying word: "heatedly." This moves a discussion to a new level, and involves emotion, which is usually negative. The word "quarrel" is similar in that it's described as "angry." This is another escalation. Now the feelings are more than "heated" – they're outright angry. The definition of the word "conflict" calls the disagreement "serious" and "incompatible." It would be fair to consider a discussion as a neutral event, and an argument, quarrel, or conflict as an escalating negative occurrence.

When does a discussion become a problem? In the business example above, it can become a problem if one person is heavily involved in one of the options. He may be emotionally involved – perhaps it's his idea, so he's personally invested in it. He may dislike or be jealous of the presenter of an opposing option. He may have weighed the impact of each option and honestly believes his opinion is right. In any case, it becomes a problem when the discussion becomes heated, angry, irrational, or overly emotional. In other words, it's no longer a discussion – now it's an argument or quarrel.

In a friendship, things are different. Most friendships involve some "arguing." Perhaps you're a Cubs fan and your best friend cheers for the White Sox. There may be a lot of good-natured "arguing" about who is the best baseball team. You know you're not going to change his mind, and he knows he's not going to change yours. Yet you engage in hassling one another on a regular basis.

This is what I call "recreational arguing." It's fun, silly, and no feelings are hurt. No one truly gets angry. In the end (well, there really is no end!) the friendship remains intact and both parties tacitly agree that the argument will continue and even flourish.

Recreational arguing may involve a lot of different subjects, but the underlying similarity is that both parties understand that it's all in good fun and there's no anger involved. But remember, even in fun, arguments can become tiresome and annoying to others who must listen. Be careful your "fun" arguments don't make others tired or uncomfortable!

When arguing escalates beyond good-natured fun, that's the sign trouble may be on the horizon. What happens when you and your friend have political opinions that are on opposite ends of the spectrum? Can you talk rationally about your views or does every discussion turn heated or angry? Are election years a strain on your friendship? If you're in a group, do the others wish you and your friends would just take your arguments somewhere else? How do you handle this situation with grace? Can you solve this without alienating one another or all of your other friends? In such a situation, you may just need to agree to disagree, and make all political talk off-limits.

There are people who seem to be argumentative by nature. If you say the sky is blue, Bill might say, "Well, today I wouldn't call it blue – it's actually more blue-grey." Bill simply thrives on disagreeing. He will argue with anyone about anything at any time. My dad used to describe such people as being willing to argue with a post if no one else was available.

Such people tend to have few, if any, friends. They are not welcome in groups. At a party, when Bill approaches a cluster of people, they tend to drift away before he can join it – because everyone knows Bill can't have a simple conversation. He will turn everything into an argument. It is not pleasant on any level!

People like Bill are labeled, rightly so, as "quarrelsome." These people find it very difficult to maintain relationships. They thrive on conflict and seem to enjoy creating it where it didn't exist before. They're often not invited to gatherings. Even family groups wish they would stay home!

Don't be one of these quarrelsome people!

So how can you handle disagreement and conflict in a positive way?

1. Make a sincere effort to see and understand the other person's position.

2. Listen very carefully to what is said. Realize that there may be underlying issues that you know nothing about that impact the opinions of others.

3. Be careful not to be critical or insulting about others' ideas or opinions.

4. Keep negative emotions out of the discussion.

5. Watch carefully for escalating emotions and be prepared to smooth things over.

6. If things appear to be getting out of hand, it may be necessary to say something like, "Friend, this is something we're not likely to agree on tonight. Can we just agree to disagree and keep our friendship intact?" And then remove yourself from the situation if necessary.

QUARRELSOME PEOPLE

Are you a quarrelsome person? Consider these characteristics:

1. **You see no grey.**
    Quarrelsome people tend to see everything in black or white. Everything is either right (their way) or wrong (everyone else's way). There is no room for shades of grey.

2. **You have a narrow or distorted worldview.**
    We all have a worldview based on our beliefs and our experiences. However, if your view is narrow or

distorted, that will color everything around you. For example, if you're a liberal, you refuse to even consider the conservative point of view (or vice versa). If you're a feminist, you see everything from that perspective. If you were abused or abandoned as a child, you tend to see everything through the lens of those experiences. Understanding your own worldview and that of the other person will help you understand both points of view.

3. **You have little or no empathy for others.**
   You are unable to put yourself in another's position and see things from their point of view. You simply cannot understand or share the feelings or views of another person.

4. **You are very intense.**
   You tend to react to every question and issue in an overly-emotional manner. You feel you must win the battle, even when no one else sees there is a war. You make every issue high priority.

5. **You enjoy being the object of others' wrath.**
   You revel in being the center of attention, even when it's negative attention. You enjoy conflict and don't mind making people angry.

6. **You never back off or back down.**
   You seldom examine the issues and the context of a situation. You tend to choose the extremes and try to defend actions and positions that most others consider inappropriate, at best.

7. **You enjoy a fight.**
   You seldom relax or celebrate life. You're always on alert, ready for a conflict. When it comes, you relish it.

8. **You tend to be negative rather than positive.**
   Quarrelsome people want to cast blame and find fault. You're very generous with criticism but seldom give compliments.

9. **You are always right.**
   If you're a quarrelsome person, you seldom question what is true or false, because you absolutely know that you are right. You seldom change your mind because you don't really listen to or care about the opinions of others.

10. **You don't listen or keep your opinions to yourself.**
    People always know what you think about everything – because you insist on telling them! You seldom ask questions or make any attempt to learn something new. You need to be in the center of conflict and your goal is to "destroy" your opponent.

11. **You know everything.**
    You believe that you know all there is to know about a subject, pretty much without exception. There is no room for any opinion but your own, and you'll defend your position absolutely.

TIPS TO AVOID QUARRELS

1. Consider the needs, feelings, and beliefs of others.
2. Avoid the causes, subjects, and situations where arguments begin.
3. If you had this "discussion" before, what happened?

4. The purpose or focus should not be to assign blame. Avoid the blame game.
5. Think before you speak.
6. Ask yourself if this is important enough to argue about.
7. Don't engage or participate if it is likely to get ugly or cause anger.
8. Don't raise your voice.
9. Will it threaten a relationship?
10. Don't bring up past issues where disagreement existed.
11. Don't use harsh or abuse language.
12. Speak with respect and grace at all times.

TIPS YOU COULD USE

a. Underline, circle, or highlight the 1 to 3 tips above that you think could make the most impact if you implemented them in your life. You will revisit these choices at the end of the book in the Planning section.

b. There may be other things that you think would make a difference. Write them below:

_____

_____

_____

_____

"Never respond to an angry person
with a fiery comeback, even if he deserves it...
Don't allow his anger to become your anger."
Bohdi Sanders[39]

Chapter 9

Benefits of Positive Speech

"Watch out for negative speech: gossip, criticism, quarreling, complaining, faultfinding, blaming, and a judgmental attitude."
(Unknown)

Kind and gentle words can have a significant positive impact on the lives of others. Healing words spoken from the heart can have great value. Positive reinforcement and compliments for good work can have a very positive impact on the heart and soul of those receiving them.

On the other hand, negative words can cause chaos, arguments, unhappiness, and have significant impact on attitudes, emotions, and actions. The tongue may be small but it has the power to start fires that may be very difficult to put out. The negative impact of our words can have devastating consequences.

However, well-chosen words have great healing power. Choosing the right words requires some thought and the proper evaluation of what we are about to say. We must exercise wisdom in choosing our words.

Positive words have healing power

If you have a good life, the world expects you to share your blessings with others who are less fortunate. One way to do that is with kind and uplifting speech. Such conduct will not only benefit those to whom you speak but bring you happiness knowing that you have blessed someone else. There is great joy in lifting the spirits of those who need a kind and caring word.

Ask yourself the following questions:

- When is the last time you shared a kind word with a friend?
- What opportunity can you see to lift up someone who is experiencing difficult times?
- Who has done good work that you could compliment?
- When is the last time you said something nice to your spouse or significant other?

Bring joy and light.

Nothing is more hurtful then gossip, finding fault, and negative speech. If you gossip or criticize someone you are denying yourself the opportunity to be an instrument of joy. If you bring the power of positive words and positive thinking, even those in the middle of difficulties can be encouraged.

Gentle and loving words can extinguish the fires of grief, discouragement, sickness, and disappointment. People need to know someone cares. When you share the burdens of others you not only help them but bring great joy to your own soul.

Speak truth.

Our speech needs to be truthful. Lies will destroy the credibility of our speech no matter how well intentioned they are. We must be humble servants of our words knowing they can have great impact on others. We should demonstrate integrity in our speech.

Others are won over by gentle and caring words that center on the truth. If you base your life on truth, your words should demonstrate that commitment.

The world needs positive speech.

By using positive words and implementing corresponding actions we establish an environment of positive thinking and caring actions that can change the world around us. Positive speech will set in motion thoughts and actions that will improve the nature of our lives. We can make positive change in the world through positive, loving, and gracious speech.

SUMMARY - Tips For Uplifting Speech

1. Think before you speak.
2. Consider your purpose for speaking.
3. Be intentional when you speak.
4. Know your audience.

5. Don't cause hurt feelings because you didn't think about who is in your audience.
6. Don't speak unless you have something worthwhile to say.
7. Don't cause unnecessary disruption with your choice of words.
8. Listen before you speak. Practice waiting to speak.
9. Silence can be golden!
10. Truth is always a winner. Don't embellish.
11. Lies will be discovered.
12. Focus on generating understanding, not on winning.
13. Conversations are not competitions.
14. Find Solutions to problems.
15. Focus on the real issues.

SUMMARY – Advantages of Positive Speech

- You appear friendly and open.

- You are easy to talk to.

- You draw people to you rather than drive them away.

- You feel good about yourself, and others like you.

- You can motivate others and gain their cooperation.

- You are an attractive candidate for friendship.

- You can be confident in what you say because you have thought about it.

These are all significant and positive results. Is there anything in this list you would not want? In my opinion "motivating others and gaining their cooperation" is a significant life skill. If I could only select one of these results, this is the one I would choose because I think it will have a much bigger impact on my quality of life. Which one would you choose? Does one of these have more meaning to you than the others? These are all good reasons for positive speech.

Be positive, people will love you for it!

TIPS YOU COULD USE

a. Underline, circle, or highlight the 1 to 3 tips from the "Rules" and "Summary" sections above that you think could make the most impact if you implemented them in your life. You will revisit these choices at the end of the book in the Planning section.

b. There may be other things that you think would make a difference. Write them below:

_____

_____

_____

_____

Chapter 10

Planning Part 1
Life Analysis

———

SPEECH LIFE PRINCIPLE:
Guard your speech.

INTRODUCTION

The objective of this Analysis chapter is to survey your life situation for information that will be used in later chapters to identify your core values, life priorities, commitments, and goals. In Chapter 13 we will formulate action steps to make guarding your speech a reality in your life.

If you have already read one of the other books in this series and completed the Life Analysis in that book, the questions and exercises are the same, but, your answers are about a different subject. However, some of your responses will be the same or similar and you might want to have that book handy as you complete this Life Analysis.

Most of us have never done any kind of extensive self-examination and certainly not thought about writing down the results. I can tell you personally there is much to be gained from writing them down rather than just thinking, talking, or meditating about them. It will give you a clear picture of your life and help you evaluate what you really want to accomplish.

The focus of this book is to address <u>one</u> particular topic in your life. It is not a complete life plan. A complete and detailed Life Plan is the subject of our *Life Planning Handbook*. See the "Next Steps" page at the end of this book for more information.

Our life planning process has five primary parts which we will cover in the following chapters.

Chapter 10, Part 1 – Life Analysis: What is your life situation today?
Chapter 11, Part 2 – Life Values: What is important to you?
Chapter 12, Part 3 – Life Principle Goals: What are your objectives?
Chapter 13, Part 4 – Action Steps: How do you get from where you are today to your goals?
Chapter 14, Part 5 – Ongoing Progress Review: How are you doing?

Life planning is not a difficult process. It will certainly be easier for those who have thought about these questions before. You might even have an existing plan of some kind. If so, this will be a good check on where you are and how you are doing. If you have a plan, it would be worthwhile pulling it out as you progress through the remaining parts of this book.

"If you don't know where you're going, any path will get you there!"

I don't know the source of this quote but I have had it emblazoned in my brain since my college days. I think it came from one of my college business classes or textbooks. I have heard it repeated a number of times over the years, primarily because it is so true.

If you don't know your destination, then any choice of roads at all the forks in life will be an acceptable choice. It won't really matter which road you take because you don't have a destination in mind anyway. And when you get there you won't know you have arrived.

We need a purpose, a destination, and priorities so we are not wandering aimlessly through life. Even if you are not a "planning person," be assured we will walk you through every step. Knowing your path is important because:

1) Every path leads somewhere.

2) The life-road on which you are traveling, the direction in which you are heading, and your expected destination <u>will</u> determine your life.

3) You cannot allow apathy, other people, or chance to determine either your path or your destination.

Without purpose and direction it is difficult to make good choices. Just thinking about the questions we will ask in the following process will be helpful. Our planning process should produce these positive results:

- it will create focus, attention, and desire,
- it will cause action – doing something,
- it will begin to establish the importance of what you believe,
- it will help you make better decisions,
- it will help reduce distractions and hindrances, and
- it will motivate you.

"Good words are worth much and cost little."
George Herbert[40]

LIFE ANALYSIS – KNOW YOURSELF

The first step in any form of life planning is to know and understand where you are today. What is your current situation? What is impacting your decisions and ultimately your life today? The first objective will be to identify your present situation and circumstances. Before we begin, take note of the following suggestions:

1. During this process you may find that you draw a blank on a particular question. If that happens, move on to the next question and return to the unanswered ones at a later time.

2. These questions relate specifically to the Speech Life Principle which is focused on being careful how we choose our words. If that limited scope makes it difficult to answer any particular question, then answer from a broader life perspective if you think it would be helpful. If the question doesn't apply in any significant way, leave it blank.

3. You might find it convenient to write your initial responses in a separate notebook or computer and transfer that information to this book after you have thought about it and modified it to accurately reflect your thoughts and circumstances. Regardless of how you develop your answers, keep your notes, as they may be useful at a later date.

4. Remember, you are developing a plan focused on the Speech Life Principle, not on your life in general. Therefore, your responses should be focused on that subject.

KNOW YOURSELF – Interests

INSTRUCTION: What are the things and activities you love to do? What gives you joy as related to the Speech Life Principle?

1.

_____

2.

_____

3.

_____

4.

_____

5.

_____

KNOW YOURSELF – Skills

INSTRUCTION: What are your greatest physical or mental skills and abilities related to the Speech Life Principle?

1.

_____

2.

_____

3.

_____

4.

_____

5.

_____

KNOW YOURSELF – Strengths

INSTRUCTION: What are your strengths, special skills, and passions in regard to the Speech Life Principle?

1.

_____

2.

_____

3.

_____

4.

_____

5.

_____

KNOW YOURSELF – Weaknesses

INSTRUCTION: What are your weaknesses in regard to the Speech Life Principle?

1.

_____

2.

_____

3.

_____

4.

_____

5.

_____

6.

_____

KNOW YOURSELF – Roadblocks

Who or what things do you fear the most? What are the roadblocks, distractions, and hindrances that might prevent you from improving your life in any way? Circle any that might apply and add your own in the empty boxes.

Disabilities	Failure	Bankruptcy	Divorce	Loss of job
Public speaking	Confrontation	War	Loss of friends	Peer pressure
Poor health	My boss	Guilt	No legacy	God
Time	Apathy	Relationships	Death	Family
Inability to stand firm	Immoral behavior	Unethical behavior	Lack of skills and abilities	Emotions and feelings
Fears and insecurities	Lack purpose in life	Lack of Core values	Lack of patience	Improper motives
Bad habits				

INSTRUCTION: Based on what you circled above, record any <u>serious</u> roadblocks or hindrances that could prevent you from achieving the Speech Life Principle. Indicate the reason they are roadblocks.

1.

_____

2.

_____

3.

_____

4.

_____

KNOW YOURSELF – Character

How would you evaluate your personal character? Do you have any serious character flaws (your religious friends might refer to these as sins)? If you have any serious character flaws in your life, you may need to deal with them in order to make real progress toward the Speech Life Principle objective.

INSTRUCTION: Circle the positive traits which you lack and the existence of character flaws that might hinder your ability to achieve the Speech Life Principle.

LACK OF POSITIVE CHARACTER TRAITS:				
Honesty	Kindness	Caring	Forgiving	Goodness
Hopeful	Humility	Dependable	Loving	Diligence
Respectful	Godly	Patient	Generous	Satisfied
Peace	Merciful	Trustworthy	Self-controlled	Thankful
Devout	Disciplined	Obedient	Gentle	Prudent
Sincerity	Fair/Just	Grateful		
EXISTING CHARACTER FLAWS:				
Bad language	Boastfulness	Gossip	Slanderous	Lying
Cheating	Stubbornness	Anger	Hostility	Fear
Foolishness	Mischievousness	Rebellion	Hypocrisy	Envy
Unruliness	Ingratitude	Pride	Immorality	Addictions
Jealousy	Bitterness	Hatred	Unforgiving	Shame
respect	Deceitfulness	Deceit	Vanity	Revenge

The above list is not exhaustive. If there are other issues you should add, write them in the empty boxes above.

INSTRUCTION: Review the issues you have identified and list anything below that could <u>seriously</u> hinder achieving the Speech Life Principle. List the issue and how it would negatively impact your ability to achieve your objectives.

1.

_____

_____

2.

_____

_____

3.

_____

_____

KNOW YOURSELF – Conclusion

This concludes your information gathering. You should now have at your fingertips a good overview of who you are and what might impact your ability to achieve the Speech Life Principle, both good and bad.

The next step in the process of knowing yourself is to use this information to determine your core values, life priorities, and life commitments.

Chapter 11

Planning Part 2
Life Values

———

SPEECH LIFE PRINCIPLE:
Guard your speech.

CORE VALUES

What are the standards by which you live? What values do you cherish? What do you believe in? What values or standards will you absolutely not compromise or violate? The latter are your *core values*.

Self-assessment and full understanding of yourself and your environment must begin with identifying and knowing your core values. Core values are the principles, standards, or beliefs that are so important to you that you would not violate them. They will dictate your most important decisions and help you choose your direction.

You don't need to have your whole life figured out, but you do need to know what matters most to you. You need to know your ethical and moral standards. What issues or actions do you believe in so strongly that you would be deeply ashamed if you violated them? These are values and principles you believe in and live by, and to the best of your ability you will not forsake them. They represent who you really are. They are your core values.

If you are a religious person you might have a core value that indicates you would stand firm on your religious principles, and you might name them. If you love and seek intellectual improvement you might have a core value related to seeking and gaining knowledge and wisdom. If you are a dedicated parent you probably have core values related to your children or parenting.

Core values may change or become more or less important as you age and the path of your life journey changes.

You may be aware of several of your core values but you probably have never written them down. This exercise will be an important step in understanding yourself and what is important to you.

If this is a new subject for you, you might start by looking at all the topics on the "Life Planning Series" page (prior to Chapter 1) and determine if any of those subjects represent core values for you. There are other subjects that might be appropriate for you to consider, for example: wisdom, influence, health, leadership, security, fitness, family, volunteer service, ethics, joy, relationships, moderation, balance, justice/injustice, addictions, laws, safety, etc.

Your core values should cover the things that are important to you. For example, you might have a core value of: "I will always try to do what is right and I will teach my children to do what is right, even if it is uncomfortable." Or, you might have a core value related to money: "I will never spend more than I earn. I will pay off credit cards monthly."

FINAL CORE VALUES

Develop these values based on a total life perspective, not just the Speech Life Principle, and make them work for you. If you have never thought about this before, we recommend you begin with 5 to 8, but no more than 12. This is a critical step in this planning exercise, so spend sufficient time thinking and evaluating your final choices. Remember, core values are those values or standards that you will absolutely not compromise or violate.

INSTRUCTION: Develop your list of core values and record them here. We suggest you try to list twelve and then cut the list back to the best 5 to 8.

1. _____

2. _____

3. _____

4. _____

5. _____

6. _____

7. _____

8. _____

9. _____

10. _____

11. _____

12. _____

Do any of the core values you listed above relate to your speech? If not, do you need one? You may not, but don't leave it off because you overlooked the obvious. You may want to include one in order to give your objectives for the Speech Life Principle more focus and importance at this time.

LIFE VALUES: Priorities (initial list)

Our perspective in this exercise is your total life, not just the Speech Life Principle.

What are the things that are very important to you today? What are your life priorities? Where do you currently spend your money and your time? What do you spend your life doing and thinking about? For this initial list of priorities, ignore anything new that you may be considering relative to living a better life. Record just your priorities today (the good and the bad).

If you do something daily or regularly, then it is probably a priority. If you average more than an hour a day doing something, it's also probably a priority. What do you regularly spend money on? Assuming you have a normal 8:00 – 5:00 job, what do you do in the evenings and on weekends?

You might have Life Priorities related to your spiritual life, the educational system where you live, the ethical standards of your friends, your health and diet, hobbies and activities, raising your children, your marriage, your times of pleasure and relaxation, politics, volunteer service, your work ethic, saving money, immorality, your job or career, where you will live, your personal growth, etc.

INSTRUCTION: What are your actual top 6 to 12 life priorities today? Record them here based on a total life perspective.

1.

_____

2.

_____

3.

_____

4.

_____

5.

_____

6.

_____

7.

_____

8.

_____

9.

_____

10.
_____

11.
_____

12.
_____

ISSUES – URGENCY:
If you learned that you had only two years of life left, what impact would that have on your Life Priorities? How might they change?

_____

_____

_____

_____

_____

_____

ISSUES – SACRIFICES AND RISKS:
What new risks or sacrifices would you have to make in order to accomplish the Speech Life Principle? Would that change your current Life Priorities?

_____

_____

_____

_____

_____

ISSUES – KNOWING YOURSELF:
Look back over the "Life Analysis – Know Yourself" and determine if there is anything that should change or be added to your Life Priorities.

_____

_____

_____

_____

_____

ISSUES – LIVING A BETTER LIFE:
Given a desire to adopt the Speech Life Principle for your life, what new priorities would you need to adopt? Ask yourself what you must absolutely do in order to successfully live a better life. What new priorities does that create and how would any existing priorities have to change?

_____

_____

_____

_____

_____

_____

_____

_____

FINAL LIFE PRIORITIES

Prepare a complete list below of your new and revised total Life Priorities. Try to keep this list at 6 to 8, but no more than 12. You should intentionally include priorities that relate to the Speech Life Principle.

1.
_____

2.
_____

3.
_____

4.
_____

5.
_____

6.
_____

7.
_____

8.
_____

9.
_____

10.
_____

11.
_____

12.
_____

LIFE COMMITMENTS

Are these Commitments the same as Life Priorities? No! Your Life Priorities identify the _things that are very important_ to you, while Life Commitments are _things you must do_ to make Life Priorities a reality in your life. Life Commitments are sometimes useful if they focus on areas where you have particular difficulties.

It's very possible that there are new commitments you must make that are not directly related to the Speech Life Principle. For example, if your desire is to be honest you will also have to commit to being trustworthy, dependable, reliable, and loyal. If you want to be generous, then you can't love money. If you desire to guard your speech, then you cannot be out of control and let anger control your tongue. If you are going to live a life free of drugs, then you must commit to eliminating friends and associates who use drugs.

The point of these examples is to demonstrate that if you are serious about the Speech Life Principle, then automatically there will be other related commitments necessary to be successful. You could have a commitment that says you are going to commit to guarding your speech, but that doesn't really provide you with much help. If you tend to talk too much in your work environment, then a commitment to let co-workers speak first becomes a more meaningful commitment. If your difficulty with speech is centered around the dating scene, make your commitments relative to that environment. Try making your commitments specific enough that they will be useful to you.

The important concept to recognize is that the Speech Life Principle will *automatically* require committing to one or more other behaviors and traits that are related to speech and may be troublesome if not an area of focus.

Since Life Priorities inherently identify your objectives, examine those priorities and determine the related commitments that you must make in order to achieve each Life Priority. The focus should be on what you must commit to in order to achieve the Speech Life Principle.

INSTRUCTION: List the traits, behaviors, activities, or habits that you must manage or control in order for <u>you</u> to achieve the Speech Life Principle (one or two words).

1. _____

2. _____

3. _____

4. _____

5. _____

6. _____

7. _____

8. _____

9. _____

10. _____

FINAL LIFE COMMITMENTS

INSTRUCTION: Based on the above, develop the Life Commitments you feel you should make in order to successfully achieve the Speech Life Principle. These should be significant commitments, therefore, select the 4 to 8 that would really help you in guarding your speech

There's a difference between interest and commitment.
When you are interested in doing something,
you do it only when it's convenient.
When you're committed to something,
you accept no excuses, only results.
Kenneth Blanchard[41]

1.

_____

2.

_____

3.

_____

4.

_____

5.

_____

_____

6.

_____

_____

7.

_____

_____

8.

_____

_____

Chapter 12

Planning Part 3
Life Goals

———

SPEECH LIFE PRINCIPLE
Guard your speech.

*"Life takes on meaning when you become motivated,
set goals and charge after them
in an unstoppable manner."*
Les Brown[42]

Our Life Goal in this book is the Speech Life Principle: *I will guard my speech.* A complete plan would have other goals, but in this book we are focused only on one goal: guarding your speech.

If it would be useful for you, you may want to note or record other Life Goals you already have or you want to make given the material you have read in this book.

Life Goals are your objectives for the future. They are influenced by your Core Values, Life Priorities, and your Life Commitments.

LIFE GOALS

INSTRUCTION: We have entered the Speech Life Principle goal, and you may list other personal goals, if you like.

1. *I will guard my speech, choosing my words carefully.*

OTHERS (for future use):

2.

_____

3.

_____

4.

_____

5.

_____

6.

_____

Your ability to discipline yourself to set clear goals, and then to work toward them every day, will do more to guarantee your success than any other single factor.
Brian Tracy[43]

Chapter 13

Planning Part 4
Action Steps

———

SPEECH LIFE PRINCIPLE:
Guard your speech.

If you want something to happen,
you will need to take action.

INTRODUCTION

All the work in the previous chapters has given you a
wealth of knowledge about where you are today and what
you want to achieve in the future. You have even written it
down. This is the point at which you actually take the step
to determine what you are going to do about it.

As you think about what you need to do, include language
that would allow you to measure your success or progress,
if possible. Where appropriate, include the dates when
you intend to begin and complete each step. The best

action steps are those that can be measured, allowing you to easily evaluate your progress.

In most cases the Life Principle involved will dictate the nature of the action steps you will want to take. For example, if the goal is to guard your speech, having an action step that says, "I will choose my words carefully" is good but probably too general in nature. Think about specific situations that will likely arise for you where it would be easy to speak without thinking. You might begin by listing the people or groups where guarding your speech is particularly important:

- spouse
- boss
- client
- friend(s)

If your primary concern is your boss, then only develop action steps for guarding your speech around your boss. When you develop your action steps, concentrate on the areas that cause you difficulty. Don't bother with areas where you don't really have a problem.

ACTION STEPS – FIRST DRAFT

Following is a list of subjects for developing your action steps. You can do all of them or just those that you expect will produce the results you want. Your ultimate objective is to end up with 1 to 6 action steps you intend to implement in your life. You will have other actions (maybe a large number) on your initial list, but the ultimate goal is

4 to 6 good steps that you are confident will have a significant impact on achieving your objectives.

IMPORTANT: Produce as many good ideas as possible in this initial listing process. These additional thoughts may be useful at a later date.

ACTION STEPS – Initial List

INSTRUCTION: Do each of the following in order to produce an initial list of actions steps for making the Speech Life Principle a reality in your life. After you produce this initial list you will consolidate and remove the ideas that are not on target. We suggest doing this initial list in a separate notebook or on your tablet or computer.

Step #1 – TIPS FOR IMPROVEMENT

You have done much of the work for utilizing the tips we have discussed. In chapters 3 through 9 we provided tips on how you might improve a particular character trait. You were asked to highlight 1 to 3 suggestions you thought might work best for you and to list any other thoughts you had that would improve that trait.

Go back through the entire list of tips you chose and the ideas you added and select the ones you might actually want to use as action steps. Select the ones that would have the most positive impact on the Speech Life Principle.

Choose the best 4 to 12 tips, and write them in the space below in any order. [The tips are located on pages 23, 37, 51, 62, 69, 75, 83, and 88].

TIPS:

1.

_____

2.

_____

3.

_____

4.

_____

5.

_____

6.

_____

7.

_____

8.

_____

9.

_____

10.

_____

11.

_____

12.

_____

CHOOSE THE BEST TIPS:

From the list above, choose the top 4 to 6 tips and list them in priority order:

1.

_____

2.

_____

3.

_____

4.

_____

5.

_____

6.

_____

Make one or more of these tips the first entries on your to your master list of Initial Action Steps.

Step #2 – IMPLEMENTATION TECHNIQUES

It will be helpful for you to think about implementation techniques before you begin determining your final action steps. These are techniques you can utilize to help you achieve your goals. You might automatically mentally use some of these concepts when you are developing and working your plan. But if they are not already second nature to you, they could be part of your action steps.

Be Intentional. If you are going to accomplish anything of value, change some part of your life, or achieve a goal, you will need both discipline and intentionality. Developing a plan and even writing down action steps will accomplish very little unless you actually follow through. You must be committed, disciplined, and intentionally do what's necessary.

Be open to change. Change is occurring daily all around us. If we are rigid and not open to new ways and new ideas, it is often difficult to accept good advice. For example, how can new ways to communicate help you guard your speech.

Seek knowledge and understanding. We cannot afford to be ignorant. Those with skills and expertise can teach us much. Seek new understandings rather than remain in a rut because "that's the way it has always been done."

Seek help. Ask trusted friends for advice or assistance.

Have an accountability partner. Find someone to hold you accountable for the commitments and actions steps of your Plan.

Recruit a fellow participant. Find someone who is also interested in making changes in their life and travel the path together. Not only can they support you, but you can help them succeed. Your paths do not need to be the same: the purpose is encouragement, not counsel.

Maximize use of your strengths. If you are making significant changes in your life, utilize your strengths to assist in your success. You are likely to be more successful if you use your existing strengths than your weaknesses.

Make good decisions. Much of our success in life occurs when we make right, good, and proper choices. If this has been difficult for you in the past, make this one of your action steps. If you need a quick review, read the Appendix titled, "Wise Decision-Making" at the end of this book.

Apply filters. Filter out of your life people, places, and situations that create temptations that would hinder your goal to achieve the Speech Life Principle. For example, if you are fighting an alcohol addiction, you should not spend time in bars. If you are having trouble with honesty and integrity, you can't associate with people who lie and are untrustworthy.

Review the "IMPLEMENTATION TECHNIQUES" above and determine which techniques might be effective for your purposes. Include those techniques as action steps on your initial list.

Step #3 – CHARACTER ISSUES

Look back over Chapters 10 and 11 and identify situations that will make your commitment to the Speech Life

Principle difficult to achieve. Also, think about actions that would make the Life Principle easier to achieve if they existed or were true. Then write out action steps that would advance your ability to choose your words carefully.

> 1. What personal characteristics in the "Life Analysis – Know Yourself" section need to be modified in order to achieve the Speech Life Principle?

> 2. Think about the times or situations when you have been loose with your tongue. Develop initial action steps that would prevent those situations from occurring or at least be under your control in the future.

Step #4 – LIFE VALUES

What Life Values (core values, priorities and commitments) require action steps in order to achieve the Speech Life Principle? Add them to your list.

Step #5 – WHAT IF I FAIL?

Do you need any action steps relative to what you will do if something fails? Think in advance what you will do if you have a temporary lapse or failure of some kind. For example, if your goal is to choose your words carefully, what will you do if you fail to do that? A possible action step might be to never be one of the first two people to talk in a group discussion. But, if you fail or if you catch yourself speaking when you should be listening, force yourself to remain silent for ten minutes, unless asked a direct question.

If you don't add an action step for possible failures, at a minimum you should think about the possible situations that might occur and know what you are going to do if they occur.

Step #6 – BRAIN STORMING

If you aren't satisfied with your list, try to think of other options. If you can't do that on your own, get a few friends to help you brainstorm the topics on which you need more input. The purpose here is to accumulate ideas, not evaluate them. You will do the evaluating later. Seek any kind of ideas! Often one seemingly crazy idea leads to a very good one.

Step #7 – CULL AND CONSOLIDATE

You should have a substantial list of steps and ideas after doing all of the above. Now it's time to finalize your initial list.

1. Reduce the list to the good and workable ideas. Remove anything you do not want to keep on your list.

2. Eliminate or combine the duplicates into similar groupings or headings.

3. Consolidate the similar ideas into one. You may want to have sub-points for the larger ideas.

4. Prioritize the groups. Within each group, prioritize the ideas.

5. Save this list permanently.

EXAMPLES

Your list might include statements like:

> a. I will always wait to enter into group discussions. I will never be the first to speak.
>
> b. I will listen carefully to what others are saying and if I strongly disagree I will speak gently and positively in favor of my position.
>
> c. I will not turn discussions into arguments.
>
> d. I will not try to "win" the discussions.
>
> e. I will not try to have the last word.
>
> f. I will always speak the truth and never "embellish" my contribution to a discussion.
>
> g. If I say too much, speak out of turn, say something inappropriate, or reveal things that should remain secret, I will apologize immediately, and take responsibility for me actions.

LIFE PLANNING ADVICE

GENERAL

Depending on your circumstances, deciding to guard your speech could be challenging and require a great deal of self-control and commitment. Being careful how and when you speak will require taking responsibility for your words and how they are expressed. You must be committed because a great deal of patience and perseverance will be needed unless you are very organized and focused.

Don't give up if the road gets a bit bumpy. If loose speech has historically been a problem for you, it may take some time to build up your tongue muscles to be patient. You may be used to speaking first and speaking a lot. You will need to harness your desire to talk. Concentrate on listening instead of talking.

KEY TO SUCCESS

We believe that a key attribute for success is self-control. Assuming you have a real desire to guard your speech, you must be disciplined in your approach to effect change.

Make it a personal challenge to be intentional about your desire to choose your words carefully and discipline yourself to that end.

If you are committed to being more careful in what you say, you must decide how you are going to go about that and then train yourself to choose your words carefully. Think about what you are going to say about certain issues, wait for the right time to speak, and deliver your words in a manner that does not offend or crush those in the discussion.

The key is self-control. Pythagoras has said, "No man is free who cannot command himself."[44]

FINAL ACTION STEPS

<u>SUBJECT</u>: **Speech**

<u>GOAL</u>: **To guard your speech and choose your words carefully.**

<u>FINAL ACTION STEPS:</u>
Choose the 4 to 6 best action steps from your initial list and enter them below

1.

_____

_____

_____

2.

_____

_____

_____

3.

_____

_____

_____

4.

_____

_____

_____

5.

_____

_____

_____

6.

_____

_____

_____

TECHNOLOGY: Consider entering information or reminders on your phone, tablet, or computer.

REVIEW

Before you finalize your Action Steps, you should step back and take a broader look at what you have prepared.

1. CORE VALUES & PRIORITIES: Are your action steps consistent with your core values and revised life priorities?

_____

_____

2. FAMILY: Are your action steps consistent with your family's expectations?

_____

_____

    a. Do you need to tell any of your family members about your plans?
    b. Do you want to ask a family member for help?
    c. Will anything you do in this plan impact a family member? If so, you may need to talk with them before you start.

3. PERSONAL COMMITMENT: Are your action steps consistent with your personal desires and commitments? Are you ready to make these changes in your life? Are you missing anything important?

_____

_____

Go back and modify your plans, if necessary.

GETTING STARTED

If you are excited and ready to begin, go for it! Begin with any or all of the above action steps.

But if you have any fear or reluctance, start slowly. There is absolutely no reason to try to do everything at once. Choose the action step that you think will be the easiest to achieve and get started. When that is implemented, choose the next easiest action step, and proceed through the list in that manner.

Some people may have a preference to do the most difficult one first and get that out of the way. That's fine if that works for you, but if this is going to create significant change in your life, we recommend you start slowly.

LIFE PLANNING COACHING ASSISTANCE

If you would like help completing your plan, see Appendix C, or go to www.lifeplanningtools.com/coaching or scan the QR code below.

Chapter 14

Planning Part 5

Ongoing Progress Review and Evaluation

SPEECH LIFE PRINCIPLE

Guard your speech.

"The life which is unexamined is not worth living."
Socrates[45]

FREQUENCY:

During the first eight weeks, review your plans weekly. In fact, as long as you have a significant list of action steps to accomplish you should take time weekly to evaluate your progress. At some point you can move to every two weeks and then monthly. As long as you still have things you want to implement, you should review your plan monthly.

We recommend you put this review time on your calendar and allow 90 minutes for your first review and update. Based on the time needed for your first review you can schedule future reviews.

SUCCESS:

Review your plan for success and failure. What can you discontinue, what should you add, and what have you achieved? Think particularly about your goals and priorities. How are you doing? Are you making progress?

MODIFICATION:

What can be removed because it has been successfully implemented? What is not working? What needs to be changed? What other action steps or ideas did you set aside when you developed your initial list? Should any of these ideas be added you your plan?

Make the necessary changes and tell a friend about your successes!

Check List

If you like to use check lists in completing tasks we have included a check list in Appendix D that lists all the steps in completing your Plan.

Chapter 15

Implementation Techniques

FREE BONUS CHAPTER

At this point you have completed your plan, including 4-6 action steps and you are ready to begin. If you want a little more help getting started, download a free bonus chapter (PDF) that provides additional help on subjects like:

- Self-discipline
- Intentionality
- Choosing filters
    -Filter what you see
    -Filter what you hear
    -Filter where you go
    -Filter what you say
- Accountability partner

Go to: www.lifeplaningtools.link/techniques

Appendix A – How to Prioritize

General

What are your objectives? What's most important considering your responsibilities, plans, and goals? You will need to be relentless in sticking to your priorities. Like your life and career, your priorities change over time.

General questions to think about and guide the process of setting priorities:

- What needs to be done _now_?
- What is most important?
- What happens if it doesn't get done?
- When do you need to begin?
- What materials, resources and skills do you need to accomplish the objective?

The Process

1. MAKE A LIST
Write a list of all your tasks. Identify any due dates for time-sensitive tasks. It is important to maintain an up-to-date list and also wise to keep an electronic back-up of the master list. Your master "to-do" list serves as a running log of what you want to accomplish over time.

2. ASSIGN STATUS / TIME FRAME
Assign a time frame. For example, this task needs to be accomplished today, this week, this month, this quarter, or this year. Identify the date you want to begin.

3. URGENCY/IMPORTANCE/PRIORITY

Identify the urgent versus the important tasks. Ignore anything else unless your list is <u>very</u> short. Choose one of the following methods:

      a. Scale Method: On a scale of 1 to 10 (or 1 to 100) assess value or importance.

      b. Other Simple Strategies

- Do the most important task first.
- Do the most impactful task first.
- Complete one major task at a time.
- Do a simple high/medium/low assignment.

4. FLEXIBILITY

Be flexible. Situations and circumstances can change very quickly. Re-evaluate your priority list frequently. If priorities change, move on to the next priority. Know when to stop working on a goal or action step. Make sure that what you are doing warrants your time.

Appendix B – Decision-Making

**"Unintended consequences rush us recklessly
through life, allowing no time for perspective."**
Unknown

Making Choices

People who work at staying on their path with their eyes fixed on their goal are less likely to make wrong or poor decisions. Why? They have the advantage of thinking about choices in advance and being aware of the consequences of those choices.

There are many major decisions in life: (a) choosing friends, (b) choosing schools and colleges, (c) choosing your spouse, (d) choosing a career or accepting a job; (e) buying a house, (f) investing in a business, etc. In addition, we make many other simple choices daily, like when to get up, what to wear, whether to exercise, or what to eat.

> *"The most difficult thing is the decision to act,
> the rest is merely tenacity.
> The fears are paper tigers.
> You can do anything you decide to do.
> You can act to change and control your life;
> and the procedure, the process is its own reward."*
> Amelia Earhart[46]

People make decisions in a number of different ways. Some people tend to rely on instinct or intuition. They just "feel" what the right thing is to do. Others gather data and information, filling notebooks with everything they can think of that would help determine the right decision.

Some make a check list of every question and answer before they decide. Finally, there is the trusted "pros and cons" approach.

We tend to favor an analytical approach to making important decisions. It requires looking at a number of different questions before making a decision. Some of these issues and questions will not apply to every question or to your particular situation. Just ignore those; they may be useful at a later time on another question or issue.

METHOD: Short and Sweet

I know there are some of you who want to make this process short and sweet. If you are one of those people, the following seven questions may be adequate for you to make a good decision.

1. Do I want to do it or not do it?

2. Would it violate a law or a precept of God?

3. Does it violate my integrity in any way (or my core values)?

4. Would it damage my reputation, if known?

5. Would it impact others or be hurtful to anyone in any way?

6. If I can answer all the above "no," then what are the pros and cons?

7. Weigh the pros and cons, then ask, "What is the best alternative?"

TEN STEPS TO GOOD DECISIONS

1. DEFINE IT: Obtain _all_ the necessary information and state the question or problem in a simple, understandable, clear sentence or two.

2. LEGAL or ETHICAL: Does this decision involve any (a) legal issues, (b) ethical standards, (c) moral boundaries, or (d) company rules and policies? Clarify in detail.

3. CONSEQUENCES: What are the consequences? Can I live with them? Who and what will be affected, influenced, or impacted?

4. RISKS and REWARDS: What are the risks and rewards? What can I gain or lose? Are the risks reasonable?

5. EXPERTISE: Do I have the knowledge, skill and wisdom to make this decision?

6. ADVISORS: Seek out advisors to provide intelligent and honest advice.

7. PERSONAL CONSIDERATIONS: Does this fit my spiritual standards? Is it consistent with my core values and life goals? Do I have a passion or vision for this issue or project? Are my motives right? Am I being influenced by feelings, emotions, fears, or insecurities?

8. ALTERNATIVE SOLUTIONS: Take time to fully analyze the information in order to make a fully informed decision from analyzing several viable alternatives.

9. DECIDE: Verify the facts, think about and study the solution, and make the decision.

10. AFTERWARD: Your work is just beginning! Now that the decision is made, monitor the situation closely so that the intended result occurs. Take corrective action as needed.

You can obtain a FREE expanded version of this Appendix! It's 20+ pages and will provide a detailed outline of how to make wise decisions.

Go to **www.lifeplanningtools.link/howtodecide**
for your free PDF copy, or scan the QR code below.

Get a Kindle ebook version for $0.99 at:

https://www.amazon.com/dp/B09SYGWRVL/

Appendix C

Life Planning Series
Coaching Assistance

NOTICE: Go to www.lifeplanningtools.com/coaching for details on the nature, cost, and availability of our Coaching Assistance, or scan the QR code below.

At times we all need some help making a plan, getting motivated, or being held accountable. If you want that kind of assistance, please contact us. A general overview of our offering follows.

What We Will Do: We will provide help, guidance, and encouragement in:

1. Completing Part 1 – Knowing Yourself.
2. Completing Part 2 – Core Values, Priorities, and Commitments.
3. Completing Part 4 – Action Steps.
4. Completing all Parts 1-4.
5. Completing your Action Steps.

What You Need to Do.

Go to www.lifeplanningtools.com/coaching and complete the Application Form.

How Does It Work?

We will contact you to discuss our ability to assist you and give you any details you need in order to make a decision for our help. If you become a client, we will set up a schedule to talk with you by phone or Zoom.

How Long Does It Last?

As long as you desire. You may terminate our help at any time. See the website for details.

What Will It Cost?

Go to www.lifeplanningtools.com/coaching for details.

Appendix D – Check List

If you like to use check lists in completing tasks, we have included a check list that lists all the steps in completing the Plan.

Chapter 10: Planning Part 1 – Life Analysis, Know Yourself

☐ List the things and activities you love to do.
☐ List your greatest physical or mental skills and abilities.
☐ List your strengths, special skills, and serious passions.
☐ List your weaknesses.
☐ List any roadblocks, distractions, or hindrances that might prevent you from implementing the Speech Life Principle.
☐ List any serious character flaws.

Chapter 11: Planning Part 2 – Life Values

☐ List your final 5 to 8 Core Values.
☐ List your top 6 to 12 Life Priorities today.
☐ How would your Life Priorities change if you knew you had only two years to live?
☐ How would the Speech Life Principle or any new objectives change your current Life Priorities?
☐ How should the Life Analysis in Chapter 10 change your Priorities?
☐ Given the Speech Life Principle, what new priorities would you need to adopt?
☐ Prepare a final list of your revised Life Priorities. Aim at 6 to 8, but no more than 12.
☐ List the existing traits, behaviors, activities, or habits you must manage in order to achieve the Speech Life Principle.
☐ List your final 4 to 8 Life Commitments.

Chapter 12: Planning Part 3 – Speech Life Principle

The Life Goal is: *I will guard my speech and choose my words carefully.*

Chapter 13: Planning Part 4 – Action Steps

☐ Select and list of the best 4 to 10 tips. The tips are located on pages 23, 37, 51, 62, 69, 75, 83, and 88.

☐ Choose the top 4 to 6 tips and list them in priority order.

☐ Choose and list the implementation techniques that would be helpful to you in implementing your plan.

☐ Produce and list your initial list of actions steps for making the Speech Life Principle a reality in your life.

☐ Cull and consolidate the initial list.

☐ List action steps for those situations that will make your commitment to the Speech Life Principle difficult to achieve.

☐ List the existing personal characteristics that must be improved to achieve your objectives.

☐ List the core values, priorities, or commitments that require action steps in order to achieve the Speech Life Principle.

☐ List the 2 to 6 "Tips For Improvement" that you feel would be particularly effective for you.

☐ Reduce the working list to only the good and workable ideas. Eliminate or combine the duplicates.

☐ Identify and list the helpful "TECHNIQUES FOR IMPLEMENTATION" that warrant inclusion in your action steps.

☐ List action steps relative to what you will do if something fails.

☐ Cull and consolidate the list.

☐ Prioritize the groups and the individual actions within groups.

☐ FINAL ACTION STEPS: Choose the 4 to 6 best action steps from your list.

☐ TECHNOLOGY: Consider entering information or reminders on your phone, tablet, or computer.

☐ REVIEW:

    a) Are your action steps consistent with your core values and revised life priorities?

    b) Are your action steps consistent with your family's expectations? Do you need to communicate with your family?

    c) Are your action steps consistent with your personal desires and commitments?

☐ Modify your plans as necessary.

Chapter 14: Planning Part 5 – Ongoing Progress Review

☐ During the first eight weeks, review your plans weekly.

☐ Review your plan for success and failure. Make necessary changes.

☐ Modify and update your plan as needed.

NEXT STEPS

LIFE PLANNING SERIES

Should you read other books in this series? That depends on your interest and objectives. If you want to gain specific knowledge about a particular subject, then the answer is "yes." If you want to improve your life in a particular area, again the answer is "yes."

We have listed the books and the planned topics again. Please note that this list will not be final or up-to-date until the last book in the Series is published.

RECOMMENDATION: We strongly recommend that if you acquire any of the books you should also obtain _Choose Integrity_. This is the foundational book in the series. We also believe the books covering the other Primary Life Principles would be particularly useful: Friends, Speech, Diligence, and Money.

The initial plan is to publish books on the following topics:

Subjects		Life Principle
Personal Character:		
Integrity*	honesty, truth, compromise/standing firm, justice, fairness	Be honest, live with integrity, and base your life on truth.
Reputation	respect, responsibility, sincerity	Earn the respect of others.
Leadership	power, decisiveness, courage, influence, loyalty	Lead well and be a loyal follower.
Identity/Self-Image	humor, being genuine, authenticity, confidence	Be confident in who you are.
Wisdom	discernment, correction, folly, foolishness	Seek knowledge, understanding, and wisdom.

Personal Relationships:

Friends*	Friends, associates, acquaintances	Choose your friends wisely.
Family	Honor, parenting, discipline	Honor your family.
Love	Love is . . .	Love one another.
Compassion	humility, mercy, goodness, kindness	Treat others as you would want to be treated.
Forgiveness	reject grudges and revenge	Forgive others; do not hold grudges or take revenge.

Self-Control:

Speech*		Guard your speech.
Anger	self-control, self-discipline, patience	Always be under control.
Addiction	moderation, life balance	Live a life of balance and moderation, not excess.
Immorality	temptation	Set high moral standards.

Work Ethic:

Diligence*	apathy, laziness, perseverance, resilience, energy	Be diligent and a hard worker.
Trustworthiness	dependability, reliability, responsibility	Be trustworthy, dependable, and reliable.
Skills	curiosity, knowledge, education, abilities	Seek excellence; strive to do everything well.

Wealth:

Money*	wealth, poverty	Make sound financial choices.
Gratitude	generosity, thankfulness, gratefulness	Be thankful, grateful, and generous.

*The first subject listed under each of the categories above make up the Primary Life Principles.

After the initial launch the books will be published in 4 to 8 week intervals.

LIFE PLANNING HANDBOOK

If you are interested in doing a complete life plan that covers all aspects of your life, not just a specific topic of the Life Planning Series, go to: www.amazon.com/dp/1952359325

SUPPLEMENTAL BOOKS
(Available after the Life Planning Series is published)

Daily Encouragement (250 short reviews on topics from the Life Planning Series)

Table Talk (Questions and answers for dinner table discussion)

CHRISTIAN WISDOM SERIES

Since the Christian perspective on many of these subjects is unique, we have planned a Christian Wisdom Series that will examine the Christian view on most of the subjects in the Life Planning Series. This series is planned for release after the Life Planning Series is published.

COACHING ASSISTANCE

See Appendix C for details.

Life Planning Series

The Primary Life Principles

Read these books if you want to live a better life.

LIFE PLANNING HANDBOOK	**A Life Plan will shape your life journey!** The next step in your life planning.
CHOOSE FRIENDS WISELY	**Life Principle:** Choose your friends wisely.
CHOOSE INTEGRITY	**Life Principle:** Be honest, live with integrity, and base your life on truth.
CHOOSE GOOD WORK HABITS	**Life Principle:** Be diligent and a hard worker.

	Life Principle: Make sound financial choices.
	Scan the Q/R code to the left with your phone to check on availability of all books in the Life Planning Series. These five will be published in 2022.

Note: the remaining 10 - 20 books in the Life Planning Series will be published individually in 4-8 week intervals following the last book above.

Go to:

https://www.amazon.com/dp/B09TH9SYC4

to get your copy.

You Can Change Your Life!

Free PDF

Wise
Decision-Making

[Get the ebook version for 99 cents]

We want to give you a <u>free</u> copy of:

Wise Decision-Making:
You can make good choices.

This book will help you make good
decisions in your life, career, family . . .

Free PDF:
www.lifeplanningtools.link/howtodecide

eBook for 99 cents:
https://www.amazon.com/dp/B09SYGWRVL/

Ebook

Free PDF

Improve your life!

Life Planning Handbook

Obtain a copy of the Handbook if you want to be guided in developing your own personal Life Plan.

Purpose of a Life Plan

- To help you develop direction in your life.
- To encourage you to make good decisions.
- To help build your life on proven life principles.
- To help you establish goals for your life.
- To identify what you hope to accomplish in life.
- To help you make the most of every opportunity.

Life Planning Series

Life Planning Handbook

Go to www.amazon.com/dp/1952359325
to get your copy now.

Don't wait to have a better life!

Acknowledgments

My wife has patiently persevered while I indulged my interest in this subject. Thank you for your patience.

Our older daughter has been an invaluable resource. She has also graciously produced our website at www.lifeplanningtools.com

Our middle daughter designed all the covers for this series. We are very grateful for her help, talent and creativity.

Notes

QUOTES

ACCURACY: We have used a number of quotes throughout this book that came from our files, notes, books, public articles, the Internet, etc. We have made no attempt to verify that these quotes were actually written or spoken by the person they are attributed to. Regardless of the source of these quotes, the wisdom of the underlying message is relative to the content in this book and worth noting, even if the source reference is erroneous.

SOURCE: Unless otherwise specifically noted below the quotes used herein can be sourced from a number of different websites on the Internet that provide lists of quotes by subject or author. The same or similar quotes will appear on multiple sites. Therefore, rather than assign individual quote sources, we are providing a list of sites where we might have found the quotes that were used in this book:

-azquotes.com
-brainyquote.com
-codeofliving.com
-everydaypower.com
-goodhousekeeping.com
-goodreads.com/quotes
-graciousquotes.com
-inc.com
-keepinspiring.me
-notable-quotes.com
-parade.com
-plantetofsuccess.com
-quotemaster.org
-quotir.com
-success.com
-thoughtco.com
-thoughtcatalog.com
-wisdomquotes.com
-wisesayings.com
-wow4u.com

1 Emily Dickinson, see QUOTES above
2 Abraham Lincoln, see QUOTES above
3 Latin American saying, see QUOTES above
4 Aesop, see QUOTES above
5 SermonCentral.com; contributed by Perry Greene

6 Buddha, see QUOTES above

7 Honore de Balzac , see QUOTES above

8 A large number of Internet sites. Search for "Jonathan Edwards,"
   "Max Jukes," or "A. E. Winship."

9 Holy Bible, Proberbs 12:3, 7, 12

10 Cicero, see QUOTES above

11 Brian Tracy, see QUOTES above

12 Hong Zicheng, see QUOTES above

13 Chinese proverb, see QUOTES above

14 Yehuda Berg, see QUOTES above

15 Korean Proverb, see QUOTES above

16 Holy Bible, Proverbs 13:3

17 Wentworth Dillon, see QUOTES above

18 Aesop, see QUOTES above

19 Crosswalk.com/blogs/dr-ray-pritchard/gossip-feathers-in-the-wind.html

20 Benjamin Franklin, see QUOTES above pp44

21 Sermoncentral.com; contributed by Paul Wallace on Mar 25, 2009

22 Dale Carnegie, see QUOTES above

23 Blake Lively, see QUOTES above

24 Sean Covey, see QUOTES above

25 Bertrand Russell, see QUOTES above

26 George Bernard Shaw, see QUOTES above

27 Spanish Proverb, see QUOTES above

28 *Frank A. Clark*, see QUOTES above

29 Eleanor Roosevelt, see QUOTES above

30 Doreen Virtue, see QUOTES above

31 Plato, see QUOTES above

32 George Herbert, see QUOTES above

33 Winston Churchill, see QUOTES above

34 Josh Billings, see QUOTES above

35 Jean De La Bruyere, see QUOTES above

36 Napoleon Hill, see QUOTES above

37 Nikhil Saluja, see QUOTES above

38 Unknown. Article: "41 Supremely Wise Life Lessons From Everyday People"
   By Jessica Winters, March 10th 2016; Instagram: Marisa Jarae

39 Bohdi Sanders, see QUOTES above

40 George Herbert, see QUOTES above

41 Kenneth Blanchard, see QUOTES above

42 Les Brown, see QUOTES above

43 Brian Tracy, see QUOTES above

44 Pythagoras, see QUOTES above

45 Socrates, see QUOTES above

46 Amelia Earhart, see QUOTES above

About the Author

The author graduated from the Business School at Indiana University and obtained a master's degree at Georgia State University in Atlanta. His first career was as a senior executive with a top insurance and financial institution, where he spent a number of years directing strategic planning for one of their major divisions.

In the 1990s he founded an online Internet business which he sold in 2010. He began to write and publish books and materials that led to an interest in personal life planning. This resulted in combining the wisdom of wise sayings and proverbs with life planning and the result is the Life Planning Series and the Life Planning Handbook.

The author, his wife, and two of his children and their families live in the Nashville, TN area.

WEBSITE: http://www.lifeplanningtools.com

AMAZON: www.amazon.com/author/jswellman

Contact Us

	www.lifeplanningtools.com info@lifeplanningtools.com	Website Email
Facebook	JSWellman	
	www.amazon.com/author/jswellman	**Author Page**
Life Planning Series	www.amazon.com/dp/B09TH9SYC4	
	www.lifeplanningtools.link/newsletter	**Monthly News Letter**

You can help

IDEAS and SUGGESTIONS: If you have a suggestion to improve this book, please let us know.

Mention our LIFE PLANNING books on your social platforms and recommend them to your family and friends.

Thank you!

Make a Difference

The law of prosperity is generosity.
If you want more, give more.

Bob Proctor

Have you ever done something just out of kindness or goodwill without wanting or expecting anything in return? I'm going to ask you to do two things just for that reason. The first will be just out of the goodness of your heart and the second in order to make an impact in someone else's life.

It won't cost you anything and it won't take a lot of time or effort.

This Book

First, what did you think of this book? Give the book an honest review in order for us to compete with the giant publishers. What did you like and how did it impact you? It will only take you several minutes to leave your review at:
https://www.amazon.com/dp/1952359376

Follow the link above to the Amazon sales page, scroll down about three quarters of the page and click the box that says: "Write a customer review." It does not have to be long or well-written – just tell other readers what you think about the book. Or, just score the book on a scale of 1 – 5 stars (5 is high).

This will help us a great deal and we so appreciate your willingness to help. If you want to tell us something about

the book directly, you can email us at:
info@lifeplanningtools.com.

Give Books to Students and Employees
Secondly, do you know any schools or colleges that might want to give this book or our Life Planning Handbook to their students or their senior class?

Do you know any companies, churches, or other organizations that would like to give one of our books to their employees or members?

Here is how you can help. If you send us the contact information and allow us to use your name, we will contact the person or persons you suggest with all the details. Obviously there would be special pricing and if the order is large enough, a message from the organization's CEO could be included on the printed pages.

Alternatively, you can personally give a copy of one of our books to the organization for their consideration. We would recommend our Life Planning Handbook, but some organizations might be interested in a specific subject. If they are interested in this partnership with us, they should contact us directly.

It is not that difficult to help someone live a better life: just a little time and intentionality. Let us hear from you if you want to make a difference in someone's life!

J. S. Wellman
Extra-mile Publishing
steve@lifeplanningtools.com
www.lifeplanningtools.com

Made in United States
North Haven, CT
09 November 2022

26487251R00085